Praise for *The Energy of Success*

Rebecca Ahmed's The Energy of Success *is the electrifying boost every business leader craves to catapult their enterprises and teams to new heights. The book is chock-full of transformative strategies that not only turbocharge productivity but also ignite unparalleled motivation. This book is the catalyst for serious professionals aiming to reshape their success trajectory.*

For those who aspire to be more than just leaders but game-changers in the business arena, this is an indispensable guide. Ahmed navigates the intricate landscape of success with precision, offering insights that elevate your game and revolutionize your work environment.

Consider this book not just a recommendation but a mandatory read for anyone committed to enhancing their leadership skills and energizing their teams. Don't just think about it—power up your journey to success by grabbing a copy of The Energy of Success *today!*

—Jeffrey Hayzlett,
Primetime TV and podcast host,
speaker, and author

The Energy of Success *is your roadmap to a vibrant work life. It's a powerhouse of strategies to turbocharge productivity, reshape habits, and supercharge motivation—a must-read for those who aspire to conquer success with boundless energy.*

—Jan Jones,
Board member, Caesars Entertainment Corporation,
and Executive Director, Black Fire Innovation at
University of Nevada, Las Vegas (UNLV)

Investing in employee well-being and fostering a vibrant workplace culture isn't just a compassionate approach—it's a strategic imperative that directly fuels the bottom line. Rebecca gets this. Throughout her speeches, consulting, coaching, and writing, she convincingly asserts that a dynamic and energized workforce will undoubtedly redefine the landscape of workforces, setting the stage for both individual fulfillment and unparalleled organizational growth.

—Kevin Koser,
VP of Global Human Capital Management (HCM)
Solutions, Spencer Thomas Group

The Energy of Success *is an indispensable resource for learning how to revolutionize your habits for success. As a student, I struggled to find a balance between the energy I devoted to courses and the energy I had available to be a positive team member at work. This book helped me achieve that balance. Not only did I learn how to reenergize my motivation, but I learned to apply the skills in this book to amplify my efficiency and master my productivity. I highly recommend this read to those ready to unlock their potential and take control of their life both in and out of the workplace.*

—Audrey Ott,
Student

The Energy of Success

The
Energy
of Success

**Power Up Your Productivity, Transform Your Habits,
and Maximize Workplace Motivation**

Rebecca Ahmed

WILEY

Published by John Wiley & Sons, Inc., Hoboken, New Jersey.
Published simultaneously in Canada.

This non-fiction book contains a narrative based on true events, experiences, and observations. In order to protect the privacy and confidentiality of individuals, certain names, characters, and organizations have been altered. The changes made are purely for the purpose of maintaining anonymity and should not be construed as an attempt to misrepresent or alter the facts presented. The intention is to uphold the privacy and confidentiality of those involved while preserving the authenticity of the overall narrative. Readers are encouraged to approach the contents with an understanding of these adjustments and to recognize that the essence of the depicted events remains truthful and reflective of real-life situations.

This book contains my interpretation of the copyrighted work of Bruce D Schneider and the Institute for Professional Excellence in Coaching (iPEC).

For general information on our other products and services or for technical support, please contact our Customer Care Department within the United States at (800) 762-2974, outside the United States at (317) 572-3993 or fax (317) 572-4002.

Wiley also publishes its books in a variety of electronic formats. Some content that appears in print may not be available in electronic formats. For more information about Wiley products, visit our web site at www.wiley.com.

Library of Congress Cataloging-in-Publication Data is Available:

ISBN 9781394245475 (Cloth)
ISBN 9781394245499 (ePDF)
ISBN 9781394245482 (ePub)

Cover Design: Jon Boylan
Cover Image: © Coosh448/Shutterstock
Author Photo: © Rebecca Ahmed

SKY10068714_030124

Contents

Preface

What if I told you that there's no such thing as a bad employee, there's just "bad" energy. And when someone experiences this bad energy, their thoughts, feelings, and actions are negatively affected. This "bad" energy is so destructive that it has not only taken control of you as an individual, but it's taken control of you as an employer and leader; it's taken control of your teams, and it's taken control of your entire organization. To be honest, destructive energy has even taken control of me!

How so? In reviewing the landscape of my employment, I've represented almost every type of employee on the spectrum. I've been an exemplary leader, a quiet quitter, and a disruptive annoyance—and each one of these types of employees has been directly impacted by my energy.

Name: Rebecca Ahmed
Position: Director, HR Systems and Operations
Dates of Employment: 2016–2018
Type of Employee: Exemplary Leader

Name: Rebecca Ahmed
Position: Food and Beverage Server
Dates of Employment: Summer 2005
Type of Employee: Disruptive Annoyance

Name: Rebecca Ahmed
Position: Sales Manager
Dates of Employment: October 2009
Type of Employee: Quiet Quitter

As the *exemplary leader*, I demonstrated focused energy, commitment, and proficiency. My thirst for efficiency consistently challenged the status quo, streamlined operations, leveraged technology, and enhanced my company's bottom line. My passion for diverse perspectives cultivated collaborative environments, fostered innovation, and helped drive projects to award-winning success.

As the *disruptive annoyance*, I created opportunities all day long. I led with curiosity to improve breakdowns, and offered short-term resolutions and longer-term sustainable solutions. I valued excellence and urgency. I didn't take no for an answer and directed my energy towards change, no matter how exhausting the uphill battle.

As the *quiet quitter*, I laid low and stayed out of the spotlight. I naturally pointed out opportunities when I saw them. But if they weren't well received, I switched gears. During those times, I reminded myself of what's most important. I rationed my energy to accomplish exactly what was needed. I arrived on time. I departed on time. I performed the requirements of the role while on the job. I used my stored energy to propel me towards my bigger goals because I knew my current situation was temporary, not permanent.

You too have probably experienced each or every one of these types of employees. When your employees experience constructive energy that aligns with their values and drives their motivation, they demonstrate focus, accuracy, and ambition. On the contrary, when your ecosystem screams chaos versus safety, you and your employees naturally react with fight, flight, or freeze. And when you all feel the need just to get by and buy some time, quiet quitting becomes the easiest solution.

What's the problem with these three reactions? You're not in control! Your energy is in control of you. All three employee types are due to reactions based on external factors. I could have easily explained each scenario's external factors to provide you with context. But I don't. Why? Because you can't control every external factor that comes your way. What can you control? Your personal energy.

Unfortunately, companies have been acculturated to believe that the secret to success is to teach both employers and employees various competencies addressing skills, aptitudes, and attitudes. They select from a plethora of teachers, techniques, and tools, ranging from communication courses to leadership trainings. While many of these instruments help in part, there is a fundamental issue—one that I propose is logically the most important element needed to effectively engage and inspire each and every person: your personal energy levels.

Any company that wants motivated and invested employees needs people, leaders, colleagues, and partners who can truly influence and uplift those around them, which means we need the energy to make this happen. This book will help every worker increase their own energy levels—physically, mentally, emotionally—which, in turn, will increase the positive energy of their entire companies.

Throughout *The Energy of Success: Power Up Your Productivity, Transform Your Habits, and Maximize Workplace Motivation*, I will illustrate how you can shift your energy—and influence the energy around you—to increase your joy and enthusiasm about your work; how you can use that shifted energy to transform your own work experience no matter what's going on with your colleagues; and how you can truly be in control of your own energy, and not let your energy control you.

Consider the person who feels trapped because they work in an environment where they feel bullied by someone else. Changing the bully never works. Eventually, even most school children figure out that when you don't react to the bully or you find a way to reply that defuses their reward from their aggression, the bullies will quickly lose interest in their former victim. And being bullied doesn't always end in middle school; bullying by a boss or a colleague drags down people's energy at work.

Consider the harried parent whose workday morning routine includes breakfasts for finicky kids, packing school lunches, finding lost homework, getting everyone buckled into the car, and making it to the school drop-off line on time—and then to the first meeting of the day looking immaculate and being prepared to contribute. Every worker needs more energy, yearns for more energy, and will soon discover how to manufacture more energy, no matter what your external life looks like.

Consider a workplace that feels monotonous or meaningless, or where the work is just plain dull. You feel like you are just "punching the clock," maybe until you get your degree or a better job, or because you need to feed your family, or you don't see any opportunities to better your situation. Millions of people around the world feel they must work like this. My book will help you in an extremely practical, specific way, to transform your experience of that very same job so that you experience eagerness, value, and joy at work.

In this book, I introduce five energetic success principles with practical and easy steps that anyone can take to quickly shift their energy. These insights, the assessment, and the easy-to-follow steps are preparation for empowering you to control your own energy levels and expand your ability to influence those around you. This will enable you to increase your own joy and engagement at work, help your peers, and begin to create a sustainable and productive workforce culture around you.

Workplace motivation and surges in productivity are a direct result of employees first discovering how their personal energy levels impact themselves and their teams, helping you then gauge, control, and modify your reactions to thoughtful responses. This enhances your physical, emotional, and mental energy to accomplish your goals.

By putting this all together in a simple-to-understand, clear way, it is my intention to help you take back the power to make your work something that inspires and motivates you, brings you greater satisfaction, and encourages you to feel empowered, enthusiastic, and energetic each and every day.

1

The Solution: Constructive Energy

I'm at the top of the steps, at an elevation of 6,435 feet above sea level. I see my destination, just under 100 feet below me. I'm about to take my first step down, when I have an out-of-body experience. I am witnessing a miracle. Twelve individuals are working together completely in sync. Their communication is cohesive. Their collaboration looks effortless. The diversity of their expertise welcomes inclusivity. Their execution is flawless.

I start to gain more excitement and join the rest of the crowd, all 8,000 of them. We're swaying back and forth to the beat of Jimmy Buffet and the Coral Reefer Band. We're smiling, singing, laughing, and dancing, completely present with the gift we are experiencing. I mentally exit my present reality and take a moment to reflect on my current sentiment. I haven't been to a concert in almost two years. Why does this energetic sensation feel so familiar?

Aha, now I know. This sensation reminds me of the "magical moments" I've created and witnessed throughout my career. Just this week I can recall the excitement I felt when one of my Gen Z clients called with tears of joy upon receiving her first dream job offer. What about you? If you think back on your career, what moments would you define as magical and memorable? Is there someone you admired who stands out for counseling you in a time of need? Is there a team you've worked with that has become your family due to the bond you created working on a project? Is there an instant you recall where everything just clicked, resulting in an innovative process or invention?

I think back to my time at the Cosmopolitan of Las Vegas, where one specific question inspired all of us so-called "CoStars" with creative solutions to increase customer satisfaction survey results. I recall how fostering an environment of collaboration advanced the way a major US automotive company now pipelines talent. How excitement shared by emerging leaders at Caesars Entertainment has created a lifetime of memories for honeymooners, families, and friends. The impact of these dynamic moments has driven me and billions of others to pour our passion into our work every day. There is only one single term that can describe this sensation. That single term is "energy."

> The universe is runnin' away
> I heard it on the news just the other day
> There's this new stuff called dark energy
> We can't measure and we can't see
> It's some elementary mystery
> Train that we can't catch
> But our heads are in the oven
> And somebody's 'bout to strike a match[1]

The most recent "State of the Global Workforce Report" shows individuals are quitting their jobs at a record pace. Less than a third of the US workforce is currently engaged at work. Lack of motivation plus loss of productivity are costing the economy over $8.1 trillion globally.[2] Each year, companies invest in trainings and courses, and individuals invest in self-help books and retreats. While these resources are useful, their impact is short lived.

Why? Because most of the time, as a society, people are trained to focus on what's wrong—what's wrong in their personal life, their professional life, their bubble. They will criticize, complain, and even give up before taking action steps towards devising a sustainable solution. Their response is quite understandable. Challenges will keep on coming. What's the point in trying? Something is obviously missing.

> Maybe it's all too simple
> For our big brains to figure out
> What if the hokey pokey
> Is really what it's all about?

I propose that this missing element needed to effectively engage and inspire people and organizations is one's personal energy. This book is all about understanding personal energy, both constructive and destructive. How to increase your own individual energy—physical, mental, and emotional—which, in turn, increases the positive energy of those around you to build a motivational workplace culture.

The Definition of Personal Energy

Let's start by defining personal energy. Personal energy is the amount of vigor or capacity you bring to a situation. The energy you bring to a situation is based on the way you see things. The way you see things is forged by your life history, training, and genetic makeup. You may have heard the phrase about how some people "see the world through rose-colored glasses." You may have a friend who does this, and if this friend removed these glasses, their perspective of a situation would change, resulting in a change in energy.

To bring this to life, let's walk through a couple of examples. Patty McCord, former chief talent officer at Netflix, explained Netflix's startup culture as "radical honesty." If you experienced and enjoyed this culture, you probably would respond with excitement and high energy as people shout feedback and questions at you throughout your presentation. If you haven't been exposed to this culture, it's very possible your perspective of the situation would be terrifying. Your reaction could range from fear to conflict, and even a full shutdown, decreasing your energy and motivation to continue presenting.

What examples come to mind as you reflect on events throughout your life? Has your perspective on a situation changed as you've continued to grow? One of my favorite videos that highlights a family perspective is of Indra Nooyi, former chairperson and CEO of PepsiCo, at the Aspen Ideas Festival. When asked how her family responded to her promotion at PepsiCo, she shared her mother's feedback and got the whole room laughing. Of course, her family was proud of her accomplishments! She was the first South Asian woman to lead a Fortune 500 company. However, their immediate assessment of Indra's responsibilities came from a place of family needs. In that moment, Indra's family didn't need Indra the CEO. They needed Indra the mother. Hence, her mother not only told her not to forget milk on the way home, but she also told her to "leave that damned crown in the garage!"

I loved how Indra shared this comment with the audience, as working parents immediately related. Numerous societies prioritize the well-being of their family, from the elderly to newborns. Family needs many times are prioritized above work, school, sports, social activities, and even personal needs. If you've received this message your entire life, it's very possible you energetically react one of two ways when asked to assist with a family need. You might react with enthusiasm when you have an opportunity to help your family overcome a challenge and be of service. Other times you might feel frustrated or exhausted from prioritizing everyone's needs above your own. Both reactions are understandable and can fluctuate based on the context of the situation and your outlook about the request. The difference is that one reaction gives you energy, while the other leaves you feeling depleted.

The Difference Between Constructive and Destructive Personal Energy

These two reactions are classified as two different types of energy. Although they're commonly known as positive and negative, their effects are constructive and destructive. Destructive energy derives from stress, causing your body to pull from or use what current energy you have stored. Constructive energy has the opposite effect. Rather than reacting to stress, constructive energy is the personal energy that your body builds and creates throughout the day when it maintains an unruffled state. Both types of energy are constantly at play and are advantageous and disadvantageous, depending on how you're experiencing a situation.

Let's look at the advantages and disadvantages of each type of energy, starting with destructive energy. How can destructive energy be advantageous? When an unforeseen event comes up at work and needs your immediate attention, you'll need to quickly pull from your body's stored energy. You may need this energy to address a conflict, push through a barrier (physical or mental), or even retreat from a safety hazard. Whatever the stressor, it's important to note that destructive energy can help you in this moment and can be essential when dealing with an immediate challenge or strain. The difficulty is, if you pull from your body's stored energy consistently, your energy gauge will reach empty, the way your cell phone battery does if you haven't charged it throughout the day. Destructive energy is not sustainable and needs constructive energy to be refueled.

Constructive energy strengthens your drive and propels you towards your goals. This energy is stimulating and expands your vigor to move forward. This energy allows you to be present to your needs and desires, as well as to those around you. By increasing your constructive energy, you expand not only your ability to lead your own life, but also your ability to lead others towards their objectives and targets.

How can constructive energy be disadvantageous? Overall, the challenges are minimal compared to the challenges associated with destructive energy. The drawbacks can create more risk in your life, and cause others to perceive you as self-centered, or ungrounded. We'll discuss the benefits and downsides further throughout the book, specifically as we dive into the seven zones of energy classified under constructive and destructive.

How to Control Your Own Personal Energy

Now that we have defined both types of energy, let's dive into how you can control your own personal energy. Unfortunately, no one can control every external factor that comes their way. Yes, you can prep and plan to mitigate risk, but unforeseen challenges are a fact of life. So what can you control? Your response to a situation! This moment of choice is key in understanding how to shift your energy.

Because energy shifts due to your personal perspective, your personal energy is constantly changing. This means that your energy is attitudinal. Think about it: how often do you notice your attitude shift because of your perception of a situation? To illustrate, let's walk through a common situation to which you can easily relate.

Suppose that on Monday, a financial services manager named Thomas had a great day at work. He accomplished everything he wanted to get off his checklist. His ride home was traffic-free. He walked into his home and his family asked, "What's for dinner?" He responded with delight, gave everyone hugs, and started asking them to grab the chicken and veggies out of the fridge to start dinner.

On Thursday, work was extremely frustrating for Thomas. His direct report made multiple mistakes he had to fix, and he didn't agree with an operational decision. On top of that, his ride home was jam-packed with traffic, causing his evening to start much later than planned. He walked into his house and his family asked, "What's for dinner?" How do you think Thomas likely responded?

Most respond with the same energy they most recently experienced, even if the question or the new situation has nothing to do with the previous events of the day. In situation number one, Thomas's response was warm and welcoming. In situation number two, I wouldn't be surprised to hear that his natural response was one of frustration or exhaustion: "I'm too tired to cook after what happened today," or even "Make your own damn dinner!"

Both storylines wrapped up with the same question: "What's for dinner?" So why would his responses be so different? In scenario one, it's likely Thomas perceived his family's question as a standard inquiry upon arrival home, or excitement to start their evening spending quality time together. In scenario two, it's very possible he felt completely different, even emotional. How could his family not take his feelings into consideration, after everything he had gone through that day? Shouldn't they know he had a long day at work and the last thing he wants to do is "work" for someone else?

Upon looking at these two distinctions, it's easy to see how energy can be contagious and can make or break a person's mood. What happens after Thomas reacts with irritation or exhaustion? How many times have you blamed someone else for your temperament? I hear it all the time. "Work gives me anxiety." "She makes me happy." "They exhaust me." When energy is constructive, how advantageous! Most individuals absorb this energy, which enhances their mood. However, when it's destructive, how concerning! Rather than exercising control of your personal energy, you're unconsciously allowing your energy and external forces to control you.

Why don't people naturally leave their negative energy behind before embarking upon a new experience? Because, as a population, humans gravitate towards what's easiest in the short term and get stuck in the same neurological cycle. People get comfortable and start repeating the same pattern, over and over again—so much so that their perceptions start becoming their reality. In this way, they consistently use the same energy, even when it doesn't align with their values or goals. It can even begin spiraling. How many times have you had a bad morning that turned into a bad day? How many people do you know who took that bad day and turned into a week, and the next thing you know, they're posting on social media, writing off an entire year (#adios2022 #bye2023). You might have laughed at this comment, but it's all too common. The impact of unconsciously wearing and sharing this destructive energy has a catastrophic impact on our personal lives, professional lives, health, and well-being.

So how can you choose the energy you want to bring to a situation? By shifting your perspective! Let's explore a few scenarios to better understand how Thomas could have responded to his family with warmth versus frustration, even after a difficult day at work.

- Perspective Shift, Option 1: Rather than becoming more frustrated with the traffic, Thomas could have welcomed the extra drive time to decompress on his ride home.

- Perspective Shift, Option 2: Instead of defining the act of cooking dinner as more "work," Thomas could define cooking as time with his family, a fun activity that brings everyone closer.

- Perspective Shift, Option 3: How did Thomas's direct report's mistakes create an opportunity for Thomas and the department? Thomas could explore what opportunities he could gain from his team's mistakes to become a better leader and communicate more effectively. He could have brainstormed some training moments to uplevel that employee's performance.

Each of the options listed above reflect an energetic success principle that you too can use to shift your perspective. In the upcoming chapters, we will walk through how to leverage each of the five energetic success principles. You will discover how these resources can empower you to choose your desired reaction to any situation.

Therefore, if you're like Thomas and want to come home with excitement and love towards your family, you can choose to, no matter how challenging your day has been. And, if you want to stay upset and leave the family to "fend for themselves" while you decompress in your room, you can choose that reaction as well. The difference is, you will be consciously aware of thoughts, feelings, and actions, empowering you to select your reaction and energy, versus allowing your reaction and energy to control you.

Final Thoughts

Once you understand how your own personal energy colors how you experience an event, you will find you have increasing control of how others perceive a situation too. The Coral Reefer Band started in Jimmy Buffet's imagination. Tired of session musicians, he led with curiosity to create a one-time experience with unknown musicians to produce an innovative sound. What was once perceived as risky is now perceived as genius. Today, that innovative sound attracts energetic talent from celebrities to locals, creating moments of flow for Parrot Heads worldwide.

Workplace motivation and productivity is a direct result of employees experiencing their leader's personal energy. Constructive leadership creates an energetic impact, one that can shift individuals to help them gauge, control, and modify their reactions. This simple enhancement of personal energy will lead to an increase in the workplace's physical, emotional, and mental energy, resulting in organizational success through a motivational workplace culture.

> You put your hand in
> You take your hand out
> You put your mind in
> And you shake it all about
> You've only got two options
> Having fun or freaking out
> And that's what it's all about!

2

The Challenge: Deconstructive Energy

Location: Las Vegas, NV
Date: Monday, August 28, 2017
Temperature: 108°F
Email #1: Subject: Heat Advisory—Take Action!
Email #2: Subject: Hotline Notification—Hotel Casino XYZ
Email #3: Subject: Hotline Notification—Hotel Casino XYZ
Email #4: Subject: Privileged and Confidential: Attorney-Client Privileged Communication—Hotel Casino XYZ

On Monday, August 28, 2017, the only place hotter than the Las Vegas strip was my email notification of multiple Hotline complaints coming in from Hotel Casino XYZ. At the time, I was the director of HR operations at Pinnacle Entertainment (PNK), based at our service center, or what many would define as our corporate headquarters, in Las Vegas, Nevada. As the director of HR operations, at a high level, I oversaw and collaborated with senior leadership teams in the creation and execution of business growth and performance strategies over our 16 properties throughout the nation. On a granular level, part of my role encompassed responding to a variety of Hotline and Equal Employment Opportunity Commission (EEOC) complaints. PNK's Hotline provided our team members with an opportunity to voice concerns with anonymity, if desired. If the concern was something that could be handled at the property level, local human resources took the lead. However, if a concern included HR or could potentially result in legal discourse, our service center stepped in.

Investigation Background

The first step of PNK's Hotline examination process was to conduct an investigation. My goal for each investigation was twofold. I wanted to ensure that no federal laws that apply to workplace regulations, anti-discrimination, and anti-harassment on the basis of a person's race, color, religion, sex, national origin, age, disability, or genetic information were being broken. Second, I wanted to ensure that each team member's interaction, evaluation, and performance management aligned with PNK's values of integrity, care, excellence, innovation, and ownership, from start to finish.

Investigation

To conduct this investigation, I flew out to Casino XYZ and partnered with the general manager (GM) and local HR to ensure I had their support in conducting a confidential, thorough, and ethical investigation. To preserve the integrity of the investigation, all interviews were conducted off-site, as the parties involved were team members of the surveillance department. As I walk you through the specifics of this investigation, recognize the energetic impact of each character and how their actions adversely impact their entire organization.

Team Member One: The Underperformer

The first team member I met with had recently joined Hotel Casino XYZ Park and was still within his 90-day introductory period. He applied to be a surveillance analyst on the overnight shift to align with his schedule, so he could attend school during the day. This gentleman was in his mid-20s, was soft spoken, and emphasized the importance of keeping his job to pay for his education. He shared that he had submitted a Hotline complaint because he was being victimized by a bully, and believed this bully was going to cause him to lose his job. He was still in training but was making a lot of mistakes. He usually excelled at learning new processes, but he didn't feel supported or comfortable in his current work environment.

The Underperformer detailed that this coworker on the evening shift was constantly disrupting him from focusing on his work. He said this bully pretended to be White Walker from *Game of Thrones* (GOT), and each time he made a mistake in training, the bully whispered creepily, "Winter is coming." This bully was senior to him, and as a senior surveillance analyst, his role encompassed training new team members, as well as providing evaluations on their performance. Based on the Underperformer's current performance evaluations, he would not make it past his introductory period and would be separated.

In reviewing the footage of the Underperformer at work, I immediately recognized the bully he referenced and noted how disruptive his energy was to this gentleman. He was loud and aggressive, and his energetic impact caused the Underperformer to cower around him. When the bully wasn't around, the Underperformer actually performed his tasks with ease and success. As soon as the bully approached him, he immediately tensed up and made mistakes. Rather than using his energy to focus on the task at hand, he placed his energy on the bully, in fear of his next move or spiteful comment.

Team Member Two: The Bully

After my first interview, I immediately called a meeting with the referenced bully, as he too had filed a formal grievance to the Hotline, citing retaliation. The Bully quickly identified himself as an expert in his field. He shared that he had worked in Las Vegas at some of the largest casinos worldwide. Performing overnight surveillance for a local racetrack was easy compared to where he came from, and he should be thanked for the knowledge and expertise he provided for the team.

I reviewed his personnel file and asked him about the various complaints filed against him from team members over the years. He laughed at these ridiculous accusations and boasted about being an innovative trainer, referencing gamification to incentivize his team members. He believed a disciplinary style was needed to weed out the weak and to produce strong surveillance analysts.

The Bully had been on a performance improvement plan (PIP) for his past actions, and if his newest victim's Hotline complaint was found to be true, he would be placed on a final written notice, or even separated from the company. He was angry and wanted the Hotline accusation removed from his file immediately, because he did not self-identify as a bully.

His coworker wasn't a victim; he was retaliating against him because his performance showed he lacked the skillset to perform the role successfully.

Team Member Three: The Gossip

The third person I interviewed had recently transferred from the overnight shift to swing shift. Even though she was no longer working overnight, I requested to speak to her to better understand what she witnessed as a third-party observer before her transfer. Her personnel file didn't show any documented coaching, and her performance reviews showed she consistently performed the duties of her role successfully.

In speaking with the Gossip, I learned that she transferred to escape the negative energy of the overnight shift. She voiced frustrations about the Bully and the Underperformer. She exclaimed that she tried to step in several times to de-escalate the situation and help the Underperformer, but in the end was told to mind her own business. I asked if she reached out to her shift supervisor about these concerns. She confirmed she had; however, her supervisor never did anything with her feedback and had clearly "checked out."

When I asked if she escalated these concerns to HR or executive leadership within the surveillance department, she noted that she had thought about it but was honestly fearful of going to that extent. The whole situation gave her anxiety. She didn't want to seem like a tattletale, so instead she sought feedback and counsel from others around her. She shared her frustrations with her coworkers on the swing shift. She sought advice from team members in security during their meal breaks in the employee dining room (EDR). She proudly announced that she even warned some of the dealers about which cameras and games weren't being closely surveyed, worried they might not have "an eye on in the sky" watching over them! At the end of our interview, the Gossip thanked me for looking into these concerns further and offered support in connecting me with all the people to whom she had disclosed this information.

Team Member Four: The Passive-Aggressive Supervisor

The final team member I interviewed on the overnight shift was the shift supervisor of the group. He had worked at Hotel Casino XYZ for over 10 years, earned his seniority, and with that had earned day shift supervisor. So why was he on the overnight shift? A few weeks past, the former director of surveillance had retired, and a new director of surveillance transferred to Hotel Casino XYZ from another PNK property. In starting her new role, she conducted an audit of the surveillance incident reports and noticed higher activity in errors on the overnight shift, even though the casino floor was much less busy. To address this concern, she asked this senior shift supervisor if he could assist on the overnight shift for a temporary period of time to provide leadership guidance to reduce errors.

This shift supervisor agreed to assist but was furious. He had planned evening events with his family in the upcoming weeks and now felt he had to cancel those plans because they conflicted with his new work schedule. Rather than voicing his concern or asking for those days off, he took a passive-aggressive approach. He witnessed the Bully's actions and said nothing. He observed the Underperformer make mistakes each time the Bully poked at him and did nothing. He acknowledged the Gossip's concerns but did nothing with them. Rather than leading, the Passive-Aggressive Supervisor sat back and disengaged. When I asked how he felt about his disengagement, the Passive-Aggressive Supervisor did share that he felt guilty. However, he admitted that, judging by the looks of the team, he assumed most would be separated or would transfer within a matter of weeks. His hope was that the new director of surveillance would backfill their roles, and he could go back to day shift like he wanted and would reengage then.

Investigation Summary

I continued to interview various team members on other shifts who were impacted by the surveillance overnight shift, and successfully completed my investigation. My debrief with the director of surveillance, HR, and the general manager addressed my two prerogatives I outlined at the beginning of this chapter. First, I assessed risk and partnered with legal in preparing position statements for each potential EEOC concern. Second, I ensured my debrief provided recommendations based on the energy each exhibited through PNK's values.

The Link Between Energy and Core Values

How is a person's energy linked to a company's core values? As stated in Chapter 1, personal energy is the amount of vigor or capacity a person brings to a situation. The amount of vigor or capacity a person brings directly correlates with their engagement and performance in their role. Therefore, we can evaluate each person's energy on a sliding scale relative to how much vigor or capacity they put into every value. Let's walk through this exercise together and evaluate how these surveillance team members brought PNK's values to life. Here are PNK's values and definitions:

- **Integrity:** A passion for doing the right thing and living up to our promises
- **Care:** A genuine compassion, concern, and respect for team members, guests, and the community

- **Excellence:** A commitment to do our best work
- **Innovation:** An adventurous, creative, and open-minded spirit
- **Ownership:** A commitment to lead by example and make every interaction count

After reading through these specific definitions, how would you rate each team member's performance on a scale of 1 to 5, using the following definitions:

1. Extremely Poor
2. Poor/Less than Acceptable
3. Satisfactory
4. Above Average
5. Excellent

The Underperformer

Integrity

1	2	3	4	5

Care

1	2	3	4	5

Excellence

1	2	3	4	5

Innovation

1	2	3	4	5

Ownership

1	2	3	4	5

The Bully

Integrity

1 2 3 4 5

Care

1 2 3 4 5

Excellence

1 2 3 4 5

Innovation

1 2 3 4 5

Ownership

1 2 3 4 5

The Gossip

Integrity

1 2 3 4 5

Care

1 2 3 4 5

Excellence

1 2 3 4 5

Innovation

1 2 3 4 5

Ownership

1 2 3 4 5

The Passive-Aggressive Supervisor

Integrity

    1   **2**   **3**   **4**   **5**

Care

    1   **2**   **3**   **4**   **5**

Excellence

    1   **2**   **3**   **4**   **5**

Innovation

    1   **2**   **3**   **4**   **5**

Ownership

    1   **2**   **3**   **4**   **5**

In reviewing the personnel files of these team members, as well as the statements provided in our interviews, I arrived at the following averages shown in the table.

Name and Value	Integrity	Care	Excellence	Innovation	Ownership	Average
The Underperformer	3	3	2	2	1	2.2
The Bully	2	1	3	2	2	2
The Gossip	3	2	3	2	2	2.4
The Passive-Aggressive Supervisor	1	1	1	1	1	1

When you average out each person's score, what levels of energy do you see? There is always an element of partiality from conscious or unconscious bias that comes into any evaluation, even when definitions are provided. Whether you scored someone a bit higher or a bit lower, we can clearly see the following for all these team members:

- The amount of vigor or capacity being putting into their role is low.
- The duties of their job are not being successfully executed.
- They are not fulfilling their commitment to PNK's values.

Unfortunately, what we see here at Hotel Casino XYZ Park is not an anomaly. As we progress through the year, the media continues to label our workforce climate in a destructive manner, from the "Great Resignation" to the "Forever Resignation." People are facing a universal problem with their work. Notice how I don't say that there is a universal problem with people. This distinction is important. I propose that it is logically the most important element needed to effectively engage and inspire people: their energy levels.

People aren't currently in control of their energy; their energy has taken control of them. It turns out that being happy at work is an inside job.

Emotions Tied to Destructive Energy

Let's look at what energy took control in the example above. In reviewing the energy levels of these four team members, we can identify four consistent emotions that directly tie to destructive energy:

- Anxiety
- Frustration
- Shame
- Sorrow

We will dive into these four emotions in further detail when we get to Chapter 4, "The Safety Zone," and Chapter 5, "The Combative Zone." However, let's take an initial peep at how each

of the team members we have reviewed so far exhibits the
attributes of these emotions, using the following definitions:

- **Anxiety:** Anxiety is an emotion that stems from fear, causing
  a person to feel uneasy. Our autonomic nervous system
  responds to anxiety with a fight, flight, or freeze response.
- **Frustration:** Frustration emanates from anger in response
  to a threat against you, your values, or those you value.
- **Shame:** Shame is a feeling of guilt for doing something you
  believe to be "wrong."
- **Sorrow:** Sorrow is sadness over a loss.

Let's start with the Underperformer. In his Hotline complaint
and interview, he faulted the Bully for his poor performance. The
first, and regrettably most frequent, response to stress is to
become anxious and fearful, and assume a victim mentality.
Individuals who experience stress in this way don't take ownership
for their actions, and believe others are to blame for their lack of
achievement. The Underperformer also experienced sorrow,
sharing that he felt terrified of losing his job, almost crying when
processing the impact his loss of work would have on his ability
to attend and pay for school. In both his Hotline complaint and
his interview, everything was happening to him, thus he didn't
feel in control of his actions or success.

In the same vein, the Passive-Aggressive Supervisor blamed
the director of surveillance for . . . everything! It was the director
of surveillance's fault he was working on the overnight shift. It
was the director of surveillance's fault he was missing upcoming
events with his family. It was the director of surveillance's fault
that he wasn't leading the team. The second most frequent
response seen within organizations is frustration and anger. Those
who respond to stress in this way also blame others for their lack
of accomplishment. However, rather than fleeing or freezing, as
we saw with the Underperformer, both the Passive-Aggressive

Supervisor and the Bully took revenge, taking out their anger and frustration on others.

The Bully taunted the Underperformer, knowing the impact his energy had on his performance. The Passive-Aggressive Supervisor sat back and disengaged, knowing his lack of leadership inflamed the overnight shift, causing more chaos for the director of surveillance. Temporarily, each most likely even gains energy by making others feel less than or making themselves feel more than by being "clever and vindictive." But, as shared in Chapter 1, destructive energy isn't sustainable. These energetic bursts pull so heavily from stored energy that they become temporary boosts that quickly deplete, similar to a drug addiction, exposing them to their own unfulfilled conscious or unconscious insecurities. As we saw with the Passive-Aggressive Supervisor, shame started to kick in because he knew he was underperforming in his role.

Finally, let's look at the Gossip. Her preliminary energy derived from a place of care. Her lack of success resulted in avoidance, which led to frustration and sorrow. The combination of those two emotions initiated the spread of destructive energy all over the entire property. Those who respond with avoidance may evade the issue at hand; however, their energy can become hyper-focused on that single situation. How many times have you said, "I don't care about such and such," or "I've moved on from that challenge," but really it's all you think about. You end up ruminating over the exact thing that you don't want to, and by way of avoiding the situation, you end up sharing your thoughts with everyone around you, spreading your negative energy.

The Energetic Impact of Destructive Energy

As we can see throughout this case study, negative energy is extremely contagious. The Bully's energy impacted the Under-performer. The Passive-Aggressive Supervisor impacted the entire team, and ultimately, of course, his director of surveillance.

The Bully, Underperformer, and Passive-Aggressive Supervisor impacted the Gossip. The Gossip then spread that negative energy all over the organization. What a ripple effect!

Why is negative energy so contagious? For starters, the contagious power of negative energy can be traced back to our survival instincts. Our brain pays more attention to threats; fear, anxiety, sorrow, and pain, as a mechanism to keep us safe. Second, destructive energy is blinding. As you see in the examples from Hotel Casino XYZ Park, each team member only saw the world from their own perspective. They had a limited view of their own situation, reducing their power to choose a different path and to see the total negative impact of their decisions and actions.

How did negative energy impact these individuals' professional success? The results mirrored the disruptive nature of their energy. The Bully resigned, believing he "beat" Hotel Casino XYZ Park to the punch. The director of surveillance transferred a new lead to train the Underperformer, extending his 90-day introductory period. Because he had to restart his training program, he continued to be paid at a training rate rather than an analyst rate, impacting his financial security to afford school. The Gossip received coaching and was placed on a PIP for violating strict surveillance communication policies that jeopardized the safety of guests and employees. The Passive-Aggressive Supervisor was separated for poor leadership and insubordination.

The impact didn't just stop there! In addition to the consequences on each of these individuals' careers, Hotel Casino XYZ Park and PNK took a hit. How so? Let's look at three areas in which destructive energy adversely affects a company's bottom line.

- **The Cost of Disengagement:** As shared in Chapter 1, the percentage of actively disengaged employees cost the economy over $8.1 trillion globally in 2021.[1]

- **Turnover Costs:** The cost of turnover per employee varies by organization, but as a whole, it is estimated that turnover costs totaled around $2.4 trillion in 2021.[2]

- **Healthcare Costs:** Finally, in addition to these astronomical costs, there is one further expense most organizations forget to account for when calculating the cost of destructive energy on their organization: healthcare costs. During my growth at PNK, I had the opportunity to oversee the health and wellness area. In reviewing our benefit statements, I learned we spent over $1 million dollars a week on employee healthcare. Shocked by this number, I partnered with our benefits provider to better understand where and how we could create shifts in our culture to positively impact the health and wellness of our employees, as well as reduce healthcare costs. In our evaluation, we identified a direct correlation between stress and medical bills.

Negative energy is destructive to an individual's productivity and health and is monetarily one of the most expensive costs for an organization. Armed with this information, how can you create energetic shifts to increase your own energy, as well as the energy of those around you? To start, I assert that the responsibility is on the individual worker to take on their own happiness and energy level, which in turn will shift an organization's workplace culture.

Whether you've been through therapy, undertaken coaching, experienced grief, undergone trauma, or suffered from addiction, the first step in creating change starts with awareness. You must be authentic about your current state of emotions, thoughts, and actions, free of guilt or judgment. Only when you genuinely accept where you are can you create a path forward that aligns with your values and goals. Are you ready to jump into action?

Individuals

Answer the Individual Quiz Questions using the following scale and definitions to evaluate how engaged you are with your work.

Scale and Definitions

1. Extremely Poor/Extremely Low

2. Poor/Less than Acceptable/Low

3. Satisfactory

4. Above Average/Good

5. Excellent/Great

Individual Quiz

On a scale of 1 to 5:

- How would you rate your engagement at work?
- How would you rate your productivity at work?
- How proactive are you in setting workplace objectives and goals?
- How aligned are you with your company's vision and mission?
- How energized are you at work?
- How energized do you feel at the end of your workday?
- How inspired are you to do your best work?
- How successful do you feel about the work you provide?
- How proud are you of the work you provide?
- How proactive are you in seeking out growth opportunities?

Leaders/Organizations

If you are interested in your team or organization's energy levels, answer the Organizational Quick Questions using the same scale and definitions to evaluate how engaged your team or company is as a whole.

Scale and Definitions

1. Extremely Poor/Extremely Low
2. Poor/Less than Acceptable/Low
3. Satisfactory
4. Above Average/Good
5. Excellent/Great

Leader/Organizational Quiz

- How would you rate your team/organization's engagement scores?
- How effective would you rate your team/organization's communication?
- How productive are your team members/organization?
- How would you rate your team/organization's stress level?
- How in tune would you rate leadership with the rest of the organization?
- How would you rate your organization's success in fostering a motivated workplace culture?
- How in line is leadership with your organization's vision and mission?
- How would you rate your team/organization's turnover rate?
- How would you rate your team/organization's physical, mental, and emotional health?
- How would you rate your leadership/organization's ability to energize team members?

After completing these short quizzes, you now have a better understanding of how you are currently experiencing destructive energy. To receive more information and to complete a full Energy Leadership Index Assessment™ (ELI) on yourself, your team, or your organization, you can find out additional details here: https://www.energeticimpact.com/assessments-2/.

Final Thoughts

By showcasing current challenges that decrease your own energy and/or that of your team and organization, we can now work together so you can seek and acquire strategies to help you harness your energy! Starting in Chapter 3, you will soon feel more confident and buoyant to bounce back from any overwhelm, anxiety, hopelessness, pain, or stress that is currently interfering with your quality of life.

3

The Journey: Shifting from Destructive to Constructive

In Person versus Remote
Democrat versus Republican
FC Barcelona versus Real Madrid
Carnivore versus Herbivore
Pepsi versus Coca-Cola
Microsoft versus Apple

Deep breaths! If you are reading this list and have suddenly tensed up, gotten excited, cringed, or put on your boxing gloves, you are thinking, feeling, and responding exactly as you're supposed to. Opposition entails discomfort and brings up a plethora of thoughts, emotions, and reactions. It's not easy to see the world from another person's perspective, which is exactly what we're going to do in this chapter. Take another deep breath in, and deep breath out. Let's reboot and become present with the opportunity this lesson will bring as we start to shift from destructive to constructive energy.

To start, I invite you to bring up your results from the short quiz or quizzes you completed in Chapter 2. If you, your team, or your organization completed the full Energy Leadership Index Assessment™ (ELI) and debrief, feel free to bring those results forward as well. Within these assessments, you identified some areas where you, your team, or your organization are experiencing low energy. Now that you have identified some of your pain points, the first step towards shifting your energy starts with imagining what your challenges would look like from a different perspective.

How are we going to accomplish this mission? We know that one of the drawbacks of destructive energy is that it's blinding. Therefore, we can all acknowledge that looking at your challenges from a different side will not only be taxing at first, but nearly impossible. The good news is that you do have experience examining other people's circumstances from a different lens! As an outsider, every person at some time in their life has listened and consulted their friends, family, or colleagues on some issue that has arisen. Therefore, in this chapter, we're going to take your knowledge from looking at others' situations and apply that expertise towards your own personal challenges.

To get us warmed up, let's look at a few examples that showcase a variety of viewpoints. In each of these scenarios, pay attention to the various perspectives at play, and where energetic shifts occur due to a change in outlook. After reviewing these examples, I will highlight key learnings to assist you in assessing one of your own situations to empower you to create your own energetic shift.

Example 1: Ask Before Assuming

My father is a cardiologist by trade, but wears an apron that says, "Born a chef, accidentally became a doctor!" Sunday night family dinners at Dr. Ahmed's house are a well-known treat in Las Vegas, Nevada. My dad cooks enough Pakistani food to welcome anyone who arrives, extending open invitations to family members, friends, patients, and colleagues. On one typical Sunday, one of his close friends, Amina, came over for one of our family dinners. Amina has been a regular over the years, as she has consistently worked closely with my dad in Las Vegas and in Bullhead, Arizona.

Amina's been a nurse for over 15 years and has always shared her passion for what she does. On most Sundays, she arrives perky and upbeat. On this Sunday, she came over huffing and puffing that she was just exhausted. She shared that a new co-worker, Raquel, had recently joined her team and every single second of the day was just so negative! In hearing her tell example after example of Raquel's curt comments, Raquel's unpleasant expressions, and Raquel's destructive energy, I knew that Amina was only seeing Raquel through tunnel vision. All of her energy was hyper-focused on Raquel's negative energy; she couldn't see what her own energy was doing to her. She was clearly frustrated, drained, and fed up.

When someone is experiencing tunnel vision, and only seeing a person from one perspective, the best thing to do in that moment is to allow them the space to share their thoughts and feelings. People want to feel heard and empathized with. By meeting a person where they are, you allow them the space to feel safe—safe to yell, cry, vent, and just release!

To ensure I created safety for Amina to express herself freely, I listened and then empathized. It's completely understandable that she felt exhausted by someone else's negative energy. Negative energy is draining! It's important to note that I didn't go into name calling or sharing unconstructive feedback about Raquel. I personally did not know her, and adding damaging lies to an already undesirable situation fuels negativity, rather than shifting energy.

To gain more insights and clarity about Amina's workplace situation, I asked Amina if she had ever spoken to Raquel about her incessant complaints and the energetic impact she was creating around her. This one question peaked Amina's interest. She was so focused on her own frustrations, she never thought to even ask Raquel, "What's causing you to be so upset?" I shared a bit about cultivating curiosity with Amina, planting a seed for her to get curious about what would compel Raquel to be so negative. That evening, she left dinner shrugging her shoulders and figured why not, it couldn't hurt, and said she would give asking Raquel why a try.

The next day, Amina went into work interested in learning more about Raquel's sentiment. When Raquel came in and instantly started complaining, Amina leaned in and simply asked, "Do you mind me asking, is everything okay?" Amina could tell this one question shocked Raquel. She wasn't sure if no one had ever asked her, or if something else caused her to pause with surprise, but this question created a break in Raquel's excessive complaining, giving her the space to share what was going on. Within seconds, Raquel started pouring out her emotions with words and tears. She was a single mom, her son was in his early 20s and was suffering from addiction, and his on-again, off-again girlfriend just shared that she had his baby. Not only was she trying to care for herself and assist her son with sobriety, but now she had a newborn to worry about. She was overwhelmed, scared, and depleted.

Amina's initial assessment about Raquel was completely unsubstantiated. She didn't "not care" about her work, patients, or colleagues. All her energy at the moment was engrossed in her family, survival, and fear. Hearing her story completely shifted Amina's perspective. She was finally able to see the world through Raquel's eyes.

This shift in perspective allowed Amina to become compassionate. Rather than responding to Raquel with additional off-putting energy, she asked how she could help. She jumped into charts that needed updating, checked on difficult patients to relieve Raquel of some of their pessimistic outbursts, and gave her time to check off a few priorities from her family to-do checklist. These few hours of support boosted Amina's energy. She felt proud of the help she was providing for someone in need. In turn, Amina's support shifted Raquel's energy too. Rather than feeling overwhelmed and angry, she felt thankful and championed. The aha moments Amina and Raquel both experienced bridged a gap between them, blossoming into a healthy and communicative working relationship.

What energetic shifts can you identify in this example? What ignited those shifts? In this example, I illustrated how important it is to ask rather than assume. We will dive much further into assumptions and cultivating curiosity in upcoming chapters; however, this example provides you with important key takeaways. What challenges are you currently facing that are based on assumptions and judgment? How are you responding to the energy around you? Are you fueling negativity with your own opposition? Have you stepped into your opposer's shoes and tried to see the world through their lens? Take the lessons learned in this illustration and apply them to the challenges you've brought forward in today's exercise. After you review the next two examples, we'll put these learnings into action to help you shift your own perspective.

Example 2: You Have More in Common than You Think

A company's success is never accomplished by just one person. Success of that magnitude takes collaboration, because energy is exchanged in collaboration, creating a catapult effect for individuals, allowing them to flow through ideas, solutions, and project plans.

For solo entrepreneurs, a collaboration of ideas might have occurred as you envisioned your business. For larger organizations, your foundation might have started on a napkin amongst friends or colleagues, foreseeing a concept of something different, better, and innovative. Of all the stories leading up to conception, one rarely hears of a group of people creating something magnificent when combative.

Therefore, it's natural to ask, "What happens when you are asked to collaborate with someone you don't get along with?" Throughout my career, I have received this question repeatedly. Usually it's in reference to someone's leader, but sometimes it is also in reference to a colleague on their team. "It's almost a cliché to say that employees don't leave companies, they leave bad bosses."[1] But we know it's true. Therefore, when I received this question from Santiago, a client I worked with while consulting at one of the largest pharmaceutical companies worldwide, I got excited at the opportunity to attempt to unite him and his leader, Liam, into a cohesive team.

Step 1: Find Common Ground

When confronted with someone who seems to be completely different from you, it's natural to fixate and point out every difference between you and that person. What if you used that energy to focus on your similarities? In this instance, I did a little bit of research. I started by looking at each person's social media. Then I scheduled a virtual coffee with each separately as a chance to get to connect with them further on a personal level. What did I learn? They both had a ton of similarities! How did I navigate that into one of our team meetings?

Monthly Operations Meeting

Rebecca: Welcome, everyone, to our monthly operations meeting! Today we have a full agenda, and I am excited to share a status update on our progress towards our D&I commitments. Santiago, do you mind kicking us off today? I am going to sit back a bit and digest; I had a huge lunch with shrimp curry and pad Thai. Anyone else love Thai food?

Santiago: I love pad Thai and curry! Two of my favorites!

Liam: Me too!

Rebecca: Wow! We have some foodies who love Thai food on this call. Looks like we might have to do a Thai potluck at our next in-person meeting.

Santiago: Today we're on target to hit our goals. As you can see in the charts represented on the screen, there are two departments with the most openings that can close this gap from now until the end of the year. My apologies, my dog is barking the background. Please excuse me while I escort him to the other room.

Liam: Happens to me all the time! My pup's in the background now, see!

Rebecca: Look at you two! Thai food and fur babies, looks like you two have quite a few things in common.

Now, you might be reading the above excerpt from our meeting and thinking, food and animals aren't going to revolutionize a relationship that's broken because of workplace differences. I agree. But if you looked at why most people don't align in the workplace, you will see many of their differences are as minute as these commonalities. My goal was to show that they weren't all that different in their personal life, to create a common ground in their professional life.

Step 2: Align Values

One of the most effective exercises with any team, but especially with an incohesive team, is to do a values assessment. To continue working towards my goal, I took an opportunity to introduce my "Values-Driven Solution Assessment"[2] to the team in our following monthly meeting. I strategically position this tool as a way for the team to collaborate more effectively with their business partners rather than with each other. Of course, this instrument worked twofold!

Once each person identified and defined their values, the group shared what mattered to them most. As predicted, the team saw how many values they shared, as well as how many definitions aligned, even with different values. For those who didn't share the same values, an aha moment occurred!

Their differentiators opened each other's perspectives as to why past issues arose. Rather than placing blame on each other, both parties started to take responsibility for their role, and apologized for not respecting the other's value. When adversaries have different definitions or values and these values are communicated, each side can collaborate by acknowledging and honoring each person's values while working alongside each other towards the same goal.

Step 3: Leverage Diversity of Thought

Diversity of thought is the most powerful tool any team can leverage. Every person comes from different perspectives and evaluates affairs differently. The more feedback you receive from alternate perspectives, the more you learn. Up until this point, Liam and Santiago used their differences against each other, rather than as an advantage to see a different perspective. After building a common ground and aligning and respecting their values, they leaned into their diverse perspectives. How so?

Each quarter, both teams published their progress towards their workforce representation goals. The challenge was that Liam reported out on turnover, tying turnover to the employment survey. Santiago reported out on retention, directly tying retention to the organization's D&I commitments. Both data points were important. However, the business was confused. Why wasn't workforce representation aligned on their messaging? Previously, each stubbornly refused to change their measured metric, or provide an explanation to the business showcasing how each was affiliated. Now, both started to collaborate by sharing each other's results to ensure they caught each other's blind spots and could tie their data points to one cohesive story.

After leveraging these three steps, both Santiago and Liam started to lead with their similarities when they connected. By creating common ground in the first few minutes of each interaction, their transition to workplace challenges became easier to navigate. In respecting each other's values, their energy could start to align to focus on their shared vision and mission, which we knew was the same within both of their roles. Is there someone you work with whom you don't like? Are you able to list all your differences? Activate these three learnings to improve your product, service, process, and communication.

Example 3: Get Creative!

You probably think you could never learn business strategies from a monkey. The Akumal Monkey Sanctuary is located in Tulum, Mexico. When I visited on January 1, 2019, I expected it to be the highlight of my trip. I did not expect it to be a profound life lesson that I would later share with my audiences and consulting clients worldwide.

The sanctuary takes in all kinds of rescue animals, especially monkeys, and gives them a pleasant place to live. Oscar, our tour guide, told us stories of how the animals came to be in the sanctuary. As we approached the spider monkey cage, Oscar warned us that we were about to see some highly unusual behavior.

Sure enough, we were surprised to see some of the monkeys walking around on two legs like humans! As we all huddled around their enclosure, we saw a few of them start to make gestures like they were drinking a cup of coffee. Two others seemed to be putting on invisible lipstick!

Oscar watched us gasp at their behaviors and explained that just a few years earlier, the sanctuary had taken in a female monkey from a traveling circus. "Mimi" had been trained to perform human behaviors for her audiences. She walked on two legs, drank from a cup, and put on lipstick for the shows. When she first arrived, the caretakers gave her time to acclimate. They didn't want to place her immediately in with the other spider monkeys, in case she was shunned by them (or worse) because of her un-monkeylike repertoire of behaviors.

Eventually, they eased Mimi into the enclosure. Leadership assumed the rest of the monkeys would teach her how to behave like a monkey, which they presumed correctly. However, to everyone's surprise, she quickly began teaching the other monkeys the learned behaviors she had been taught for her circus act. That's what we were seeing right before our eyes!

I laughed with the other tourists, but it got me thinking. What if the sanctuary had never introduced Mimi to the other monkeys? Over the past few years, as I have consulted with organizations across the US, I am consistently asked for advice on how to source top talent through a diversity, equity, inclusive, and accessible (DEIA) lens. "There's a 'war on talent.'" "People don't want to work anymore." "There aren't any diverse candidates in my geographical region." "Open roles keep increasing; qualified candidates are not applying." Perhaps there's an opportunity to learn from Mimi the monkey?

I love sharing this example because it gives hiring managers an opportunity to reflect on how they are defining qualified candidates. If Mimi were a candidate, she would not have met the qualifications of the role, and probably would have received a rejection email. What a missed opportunity that would have been, as Mimi's one transferable skill has resulted in the most anticipated tourist attraction at the sanctuary! Take this lesson and learn from Mimi the monkey. Shift your perspective and get creative. What has worked in the past will not always work in the future. Appreciate your talent pool's differences as much as their similarities. As people and the workplace evolve, our natural selection must too.

Now that we have walked through three examples to showcase how individuals, teams, and organizations can create perspective shifts, it's time to put these lessons learned into action. In Chapter 2, I asked you to complete an authentic evaluation of your energy in your professional life. From there, I invited you to bring one specific challenge forward that you recently faced. Please be sure to pick a past challenge that has already been resolved. By focusing on a past challenge, your destructive blinders from this challenge will subside because it's not a conundrum that's presently causing you stress.

Take a moment and write down the specifics of this challenge that you recently faced:

_____

_____

_____

_____

Outline your initial perspective of the situation. What did you believe and why?

_____

_____

_____

_____

How did this challenge impact your energy? Describe any emotions, thoughts, or actions that came into play while you experienced this challenge.

_____

_____

_____

_____

Now that you have outlined this past challenge and your past perspective, let's look at this challenge through a different lens. Do you see any potentially new perspectives that you didn't account for before? If so, what other perspectives have you identified? (These perspectives can include your own, or those of other parties.)

_____

_____

_____

How do these new perspectives impact your current energy? Describe any emotions, thoughts, or actions that are coming into play.

_____

_____

_____

_____

Are you surprised about the new perspectives you were able to identify that you didn't recognize before? Are you still struggling to see another perspective with the specific challenge you brought forward? If so, don't stress! This isn't easy and takes time and practice. Be persistent. Continue to apply this application to a variety of past examples to expose you to the possibility of detecting a new perspectives and energetic shift. The most important takeaway of this tool is that you can start to see how your thoughts, emotions, and actions are all connected, and all impact your energy.

Let's investigate this connection further, using the Energetic Self-Perception Wheel (see Figure 3.1). Starting from the center, you see there are seven levels of energy. Each energy level has a core thought, core feeling/emotion, and core action/result. As you can see, each energy corresponds with the descriptors shown in the accompanying chart.

Energy Level	Core Thoughts	Core Feeling/Emotion	Core Action/Results
1	Victim	Apathy	Lethargy
2	Conflict	Anger	Defiance
3	Responsibility	Forgiveness	Cooperation
4	Concern	Compassion	Service
5	Reconciliation	Peace	Acceptance
6	Synthesis	Joy	Wisdom
7	Nonjudgment	Absolute Passion	Creation

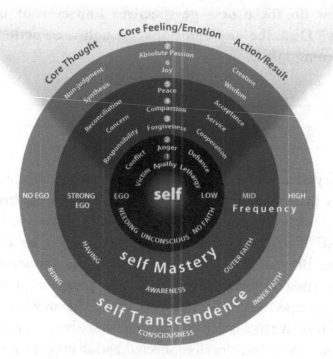

FIGURE 3.1 Energetic Self-Perception Wheel
Source: Bruce D. Schneider

The descriptors are summations of characteristics to help you classify which energy level you are experiencing. I like to think of this chart as a cheat sheet: it will become your barometer for evaluating what level of energy you are presently undergoing. In the upcoming chapters, I have categorized these levels into zones. Since each level of energy has advantages and disadvantages; each zone will help you further distinguish why you use each level of energy in your day to day, and under stress.

The next area I would like you to focus on within the Energetic Self-Perception Wheel is the center (see Figure 3.1). As you can see, the center says "Self." As you continue to scroll your eyes from the center of the circle to the outer edges, you will see that ego starts to fade. Why? Because when a person sees the world through the lens of their ego, they focus on themselves.

When you are seeing the world through the lens of just yourself, it's natural to ask questions like:

- How do I compare to others?
- How do I keep myself safe?
- How do I fight for me?

"The ego likes blaming, finding fault, making excuses, inflicting payback, and lashing out, all of which are ultimate forms of self-protection. The ego is also a fan of avoidance—assuring the offender that we're fine, pretending that it doesn't matter, that we're impervious."[3]

As the ego starts to fade, you will start to expand your view of the world from another perspective. The focus on yourself will start to dissipate, increasing the frequency at which you operate. What is frequency and what does it have to do with energy? The basic definition of frequency is the rate of vibration over a specific period of time. Low frequency attracts low energy. High frequency attracts high energy.

I like to compare this to living a healthy or unhealthy lifestyle. When you're unhealthy, it's easy to skip workouts, eat fast food, and be lazy. The feeling is initially effortless and accessible. However, what are the long-term effects of living an unhealthy lifestyle? The long-term effects feel heavy and strenuous, like moving through quicksand. This is why it's so hard to escape.

When you're healthy, you feel light, like you're floating. You might experience moments of discomfort as you learn about new foods, new workouts, and have to adjust your schedule to personal and professional commitments. However, the results are fueling, energizing you even more towards higher levels of success with ease. As we dive into the seven zones of energy and you start to evaluate your thoughts, emotions, and actions, I will call in and call out your ego. Where and when do you feel heavy and overwhelmed? Where and when do you feel light, and time flies by? Fundamentally, with each exercise, you will discover why your personal energy reverts to what you know, empowering you to create energetic shifts to confidently maneuver from lower to higher levels of frequency.

Final Thoughts

Now that you have an overview of the Energetic Self-Perception Wheel, are you eager to uncover how each level of energy boosts or depletes your drive towards your goals? If so, put on your workout gear and let's get this physical, mental, and emotional workout started! We will commence with heavy lifting, identifying what is weighing you down and where you are operating under lower levels of energy. Once we push through the resistance of level one and level two energy, we will shift gears to a flat road, unearthing where you're coasting and believe you are "doing just fine." Ultimately, we will unearth what's holding you back from achieving success and leverage five energetic success principles to propel you into higher levels of energy.

4

The Safety Zone

"You can't do this. Don't risk everything you have. It's not worth it. Stay safe!" Sounds familiar? Ugh ... feel familiar? These are the words of that little voice in your head, the one some label as their inner critic or gremlin. The voices that tell you, "You aren't good enough," reside in energy level one, the lowest level of energy a person can experience. Within this energy zone, people feel as if life is happening to them versus feeling in control of their choices and future. The intention of level one energy is to keep you feeling safe and risk free. The disadvantage is that self-doubt and fear reside within this energy level, holding you back from stepping out of your comfort zone.

Safety Zone Qualities: Fear, Self-Doubt, Risk Adverse, Avoidance

To better understand level one energy, we must start with its intention: to keep you safe. Energy level one is your security risk assessment tool. Scientifically, your brain is even "wired" with this safety built in. How so? The amygdala is part of your neural system, and one of its main roles is to evaluate your safety and alert you to threats. Throughout your day-to-day activities, it's important to acknowledge this tool and energy's use and strengths. Here are some basic examples of level one energy:

- Looking both ways before crossing a street
- Assessing your surroundings before entering a space, or adding your contribution to a meeting
- Conducting an analysis before accepting an opportunity

When used for your advantage, level one energy is essential and beneficial. Its feeling of protection is unmatched and comfortable, like being wrapped up in a cozy blanket by the fire on a cold winter day. Using this energy to ensure your safety is imperative, as it secures your livelihood to continue to the next day.

The moment your cozy blanket becomes anything more than a piece of fabric is the moment you know you've lost control to energy level one. Rather than making decisions with your safety in mind, you've surrendered your decisions in fear of losing your safeguard. The destructive effects of this energy make you feel like a hostage to those negative voices in your head, taking over your thoughts, emotions, and actions.

Remember the Self-Perception Wheel in Chapter 3? What word was at the center? Self! When you are experiencing this energy, you become your biggest enemy. You doubt yourself, you criticize yourself, and you avoid addressing your own insecurities. What's even more concerning is that this energy is so destructive, you believe you are worth less than you really are. In most cases, these thoughts stem from occurrences within your upbringing, and then become triggers in the workplace, resulting in imposter syndrome, limiting beliefs, and burnout. Let's look at these three focus areas to see how fear, self-doubt, and avoidance take control, leaving you feeling anxious, fearful, and exhausted.

Imposter Syndrome

In September 2022, I was asked to speak about Imposter Syndrome at Johnson & Johnson's Diversity, Equity, and Inclusion (DE&I) Skill Building Series with the CEO of BCT Partners, Dr. Randal Pinkett. The DE&I Skill Building Series encompassed four presentations in total, looking at DE&I through the lens of intersectionality.

To provide a little background, Kimberlé Crenshaw coined the term "intersectionality" in 1989. Its definition continues to evolve, but the key takeaway focuses on the understanding that people's experiences are shaped by a variety of factors, such as their upbringing, cultural background, gender identity, sexuality, race, and age, to name a few. These intersecting identities can propel or oppress a person, and it's important to recognize that each person's intersectional identities shape how they see and experience the world.

Sound familiar? As explored in Chapter 1, personal energy is the amount of vigor or capacity you bring to a situation. The energy you bring to a situation is based on the way you see things. The way you see things is forged by your life history, training, and genetic makeup. By definition, life history, training, and genetic makeup are all intersectional identities. Therefore, when I learned that more than 200 J&J employees would be attending our session, my curiosity immediately led me to the following question: How do the various attending intersectional identities experience imposter syndrome?

The history of imposter syndrome dates back to late 1970s, when the term was coined by two psychologists, Doctors

Suzanne Imes and Rose Clance. The common theme identified within imposter syndrome is that highly accomplished individuals are extremely concerned about being exposed as a fraud, even though they have the expertise to take ownership of their accomplishments. There are five classifications of imposters, and many experience a variety of these classifications at the same time, different times, and on and off throughout their lives.

In summary, here are the five types of imposters and how they are defined:

1. **The Perfectionist:** Perfectionists tend to set overly high goals for themselves, wanting everything to be "100% perfect." When they fail to reach their goal, no matter how unrealistic to attain, they experience major self-doubt and self-criticism.

2. **The Superhuman:** This type of imposter is convinced they are less worthy than their coworkers or peers. To compensate for their insecurities, they push themselves to work harder than anyone around them to show how committed they are to their work.

3. **The Natural Genius:** Individuals with this imposter syndrome believe they should naturally be able to succeed without having to put in a lot of effort. They judge their accomplishments based on how easy something was to complete, as well as how fast they finished the task. When something is challenging and takes time, these imposters feel a sense of shame and anxiety for not excelling with ease.

4. **The Soloist:** Soloists believe they are the only who can "do things right" and view asking for help from others or delegating tasks as a weakness. By taking on everything, this imposter syndrome usually leads to burnout and exhaustion.

5. **The Expert:** Those who experience this form of imposter syndrome evaluate their success based on how much and

what they know. They live in fear of being considered inexperienced or "green" when they don't know "everything" about a situation or role.

Let's look at some of the examples I shared, as well as some feedback provided by the audience. Samples showcase the impact of level one energy within success communities, not belonging, and the discomfort one experiences when trying something new, such as a stepping into a different role or career.

Success Communities

I'll start by highlighting my story, as I did in my presentation with J&J. While I received an overwhelming amount of feedback from other Asian Americans born and raised in the United States with similar upbringings, I know the feelings we shared resonate across success communities worldwide.

My father, the oldest of seven siblings, was born and raised in Pakistan and moved to the United States to pursue a medical degree in cardiology. He consistently graduated top of his class, and has been a leader in the medical community in Las Vegas since his arrival during the mid-1970s.

My mother was an only child, born in Las Vegas. She was raised by her mother, who worked as a cocktail waitress in the casino showrooms "by day" and owned her own travel agency with her sisters as her side hustle/passion project. My mom grew up exposed to show business and travel, and eventually graduated from nursing school, supporting herself while working full-time.

As you can see, they came from different backgrounds, with hard work as a steady theme mutually exhibited.

As the oldest of nine, I was emboldened to excel, and was proud to be a role model for my siblings. Initially, I enjoyed the support and encouragement I received to shine at school, in sports, and within our various local communities. That was, until I received my first B– in elementary school. The reaction I received for not getting an A shifted my entire perspective.

The excitement I had gained from learning and growing started to feel like a heavy burden, making me feel anxious and fearful of failure. My definition of success completely changed because of this shift in outlook. Previously, I loved trying new hobbies, activities, and classes. I still laugh at my attempt at gymnastics, only to learn I couldn't complete a cartwheel, no matter how many times I tried! After that B–, I no longer looked at trying things as fun. If I wasn't going to get that A, it wasn't worth the pain.

My takeaway was that it took hard work and determination to be successful. I obviously didn't work hard enough because I got a B–. To combat this insecurity, I worked harder than anyone around me. I defined success not just by my achievements, but by how hard they were to accomplish. How has that served me throughout my life? At first glance, most would applaud my hard work and highlight how far this dedication got me. The truth was, in being motivated by my fear of failing, I was what women's leadership expert , and author of *Playing Big*, Tara Mohr, would call "playing small." Additionally, I was exhausted from taking on . . . everything.

Outcast Communities

The second example I shared with J&J came directly from Michelle Obama. As part of her original book tour for *Becoming*, speaking to 300 students at Elizabeth Garret Anderson School in London, she revealed that she still battles with imposter syndrome. She explained that she grew up in a rural community in Chicago, and that many times, society looks at children with her background as "not belonging."[1]

When you don't feel like you belong, it's natural to raise all sorts of questions about your own capabilities and accomplishments strictly based on your socioeconomic background and the color of your skin, two of her identified intersectional identities. "I still remember that feeling of doubt, that feeling of another adult placing a barrier on me that I didn't even have for myself," she said. "The person whose job it was to help young people reach their dream saw me, and whatever she saw in me told me that my dreams were too high."[1]

Many in the audience resonated with Obama's sentiment and vocalized how this tied to the importance of seeing others like them in leadership roles. When you don't see people like you at the executive level, the inherent question becomes, do I belong here? I loved amplifying this message, echoing Lizzo's recent Emmy acceptance speech.[2] She proudly declared, "When I was a little girl, all I wanted to see was me in the media. Someone fat like me, Black like me, beautiful like me. If I could go back and tell little Lizzo something, I'd be like, 'You're gonna see that person but bitch it's gonna have to be you.'" Stepping into that role as the "first person" takes confidence and doesn't come without the feeling of being an imposter.

New Communities

"Rebecca, I can't apply to be an executive managing director. I don't meet the minimum qualifications detailed in the job description." Think back to the first time you applied to a stretch role, assignment, or promotion. How confident were you in your abilities to succeed? Did any fear or self-doubt arise? Trying something new comes with uncertainty, which many times leads to insecurities. Therefore, I wasn't surprised when I heard this feedback in 2021, when I got a call from an attorney who had recently sold his legal practice at the end of 2018. I received this response consistently from my coaching clients, no matter their age, gender identity, or experience.

In my first meeting with Everson, he explained that he had been a successful personal injury attorney in Miami, Florida, since graduating from law school at the University of Pennsylvania in 2010. He worked his way up at a boutique personal injury practice and decided to open his own shop in 2013. After five years of running his own business, he considered himself an expert in his field, and he was ready for a change.

In 2019, Everson returned to school to obtain his master's in finance at Georgetown. He gained exposure to the world of commercial real estate (CRE) through his business referral network, Business Network International (BNI), and was confident about gaining employment after graduation. Unfortunately, as we all know, 2020 was a difficult year due to Covid-19, especially those in CRE. Everson took this time to connect with his family and perfect his expertise in finance, prepping for the labor market to open back up for him to seek employment and start his new role. When the market started to open in 2021, Everson reached out to me, soliciting my coaching services to assist him with navigating through this difficult transition.

When speaking with me, Everson immediately detailed his credentials and expertise. He was positive when he spoke about his background and education and felt confident about interviewing when given the chance. The problem was, he had never applied to a position before. He was poached right out of law school, and then opened his own practice. This was new territory for him, and he didn't know what to do.

Everson's initial approach in this new arena was to apply for roles he was overqualified for, assuming those would be easy wins. Each time he didn't hear back about a role that was undoubtedly an entry-level position, he recoiled even further. He clearly wasn't an expert in this field and had heard I was, coming from a background in HR with experience in career services. Based on my expertise, he believed only I could apply correctly and get him a job, offering me an additional $5,000 just to complete each application. Of course, my answer was no, because I identified the hardship he was experiencing as imposter syndrome from previously working in an area where he felt like an expert.

What forms of imposter syndrome did you identify throughout each example? Do you resonate with one, two, or all five? What lessons did you learn in reviewing each person's background and perspective? Even though we all have different DNA and come from a variety of upbringings, the sentiments we experience with level one energy all come from the same place—a place where you don't feel safe.

Limiting Beliefs

In reviewing the above three illustrations, we identified where each person, myself included, exhibited one or more types of imposter syndrome. One of my imposter beliefs was that it had to be hard to be successful, and constantly added more to my plate. Michelle shared that she always strived to be the best, to ensure she "earned" her seat at the table. Everson's success relied on his expertise. When he wasn't an expert, he quickly shut down.

These reactions stem from limiting beliefs, which are experiences masked as facts. Limiting beliefs are stories we tell ourselves, that we believe to be true. When you break down each of our limiting beliefs, here is what you will see:

- I got a B–. That is a fact. I deserved a B– as punishment for not working hard enough. That's a story and a limiting belief.

- Michelle was told her dreams were too high. That's a fact. She told herself she didn't belong. That's a story and a limiting belief.

- Everson didn't hear back from an employer about an application he submitted. That's a fact. Only an expert with a background in HR and career services can obtain a job. That's a story and a limiting belief.

Do you see how one experience can shape a lifetime of destructive thoughts, insecure feelings, and impractical reactions? Limiting beliefs are the root cause of level one energy, and they are the hardest for people to identify. Published studies indicate that limiting beliefs often stem from distressing events that most likely occurred during childhood.

These distressing events might be very traumatic, or it's possible that what was once upsetting to you as a child wouldn't seem like a concerning event now. I've had clients share trauma recollections from rape and abuse, and others whose distress stemmed from the volume of their hair or the smell of their food. It's also possible that you might not even initially remember the actual event, and only recall the story.

No matter how big or how small, in that moment something occurred that caused you stress and made you feel unsafe. To combat that feeling, and to protect yourself moving forward, you created a story, and put on a shield to protect yourself from feeling that way again. I put on a hard-working shield, believing that would protect me from my shortcomings. Michelle put on the perfection shield, believing that would protect her from feeling that she didn't belong. Everson put on the expert shield, believing that would protect him from failing.

How does a shield serve you? Many times, it can be something you wear as a badge of honor. I wore my hard-working shield with pride, believing that working harder than anyone else would lead me to success. At times it did, but other times it led me to playing safe, or burning out. People often use their shield as an excuse to justify their actions. Everson didn't believe he could obtain a role without me applying for him. He justified his request to have me complete his applications with his shield: "I'm not the expert." I don't want to speak on Michelle's behalf, but I invite you to speculate: how could she have worn her shield as a badge of honor or an excuse to avoid something uncomfortable?

Once you've created a narrative that you believe defines you, it's hard to see any other storyline. Psychotherapist Amy Morin, LCSW, explains this psychological principle as "belief perseverance."[3] Similar to algorithms within our social media, individuals can filter in and filter out everything that substantiates or revokes the legitimacy of their belief.

No matter how much you try to justify your limiting beliefs, as soon as you don't feel in control to change the narrative, you have an opportunity to lean in and discover why. Mapping out what occurred (fact) versus the story you tell yourself (fiction) is the first step to discovering that "why."

As you continue to explore stronger levels of energy in the upcoming chapters, you will discover what tools work best for you in creating energetic shifts. But before you can make those shifts, you must be authentic with yourself and identify what occurred in your past that caused you to put on a shield, taking away your power to choose. I can't reiterate this enough: this is one of the most challenging exercises. Whether you do this assignment alone, with loved ones, or with a licensed mental health professional, this breakthrough will assist you in making peace with your limiting beliefs. In doing so, you will gain control to remove the shields that don't serve you to design your own path forward.

Burnout

Now that you understand the "why" behind the shield, let's look at the energetic impact of our armor's destruction within level one energy. As we explored earlier, when a person experiences duress and is seeing the world through this energy level, they are coming from a place of fear, self-doubt, and avoidance. How do these thoughts leave one feeling? Anxious, fearful, and exhausted—all qualities categorized under burnout. "Burn-out is a syndrome conceptualized as resulting from chronic workplace stress that has not been successfully managed. It is characterized by three dimensions: feelings of energy depletion or exhaustion; increased mental distance from one's job, or feelings of negativism or cynicism related to one's job; and reduced professional efficacy."[4]

How do you know if you are burned out? There are a variety of research assessments that measure each of the three focus areas listed above, starting with Maslach Burnout Inventory (MBI). They each calculate diverse dimensions within the three primary areas of feeling overtired, withdrawn, and insecure, all qualities of low energy.

Let's take these measurements into the workplace. When you start a new role, it's common to experience stress as you acclimatize to the culture and learn the tasks of your job. Are you currently working on a stressful project that requires more attention and hours than usual? What if you were just assigned a new leader? Who doesn't feel stressed as someone new comes in and asks questions to evaluate the team's processes and procedures? These are just a few common examples in the workplace. Does that mean each time someone experiences one of these common stress-induced situations, they are also experiencing burnout? Most likely the answer is no.

Stress and weariness for short durations are customary as change occurs. There's a "defined" period of time when you will experience fatigue, but you know there is an end date and feel confident about the stress ending in alignment with that end date. Burnout occurs when you consistently experience stress, so much so that it becomes cyclical. Rather than taking breaks to energetically recharge, you continue to deplete your battery, emotionally, physically, and mentally.

How does burnout manifest in the workplace for individuals? Let's walk through a few examples to better illustrate each response. When an employee is experiencing a **flight** response, their reaction stems from fear, telling them to "run" from a threat. Wedding planner Mauricio consistently screams at his team each time they're under pressure for a large wedding. Knowing that he targets those in his line of sight, his team runs from the spotlight to ensure they can complete their job.

Karissa, a flight attendant for American Airlines, approached a customer to ask them to please cover their nose and mouth with their mask while flying. The customer responded by yelling at Karissa, shouting out political opinions and medical justifications as to why she didn't need to cover both her mouth and nose. Burned out from the pandemic and customer responses to a safety protocol she is required to follow, Karissa completely **freezes**. She doesn't move, she doesn't speak, she just looks at the customer blankly, stunned at what she is presently experiencing.

Workplace **avoidance** occurs when a person is so disengaged from their work that they purposely abstain from completing a task. Jones, an advertising sales account executive, avoids sending his client their weekly report, fed up with his client's stubborn mindset. Jones keeps making recommendations to change their marketing strategy, but this client won't budge. Jones tells everyone he doesn't care and has moved on. What's really going on in his head? He keeps ruminating over the same conversations again and again. All of his energy is draining minute by minute, just to avoid a courageous conversation.

Christian, a student at the Aveda Institute, is **exhausted** from working and going to school full time. Rather than spending time off with their husband, they sleep on their days off, distancing them from their partner and support. Each time Christian's husband tries to discuss their exhaustion, Christian retreats even further, just too tired to deal with anything more than their current workload.

Parvati is a sophomore at Notre Dame, majoring in political science. To prepare for a career in politics, she signs up for a number of extracurricular activities in addition to her full-time schedule. In trying to balance everything, she notices she is dropping the ball in several areas, causing her to become distraught with **anxiety**. The more mistakes she makes, the more anxious she gets.

In reviewing the above samples, which have you experienced or are currently experiencing? How are these symptoms impacting your personal and professional life? More importantly, how are they affecting the health of your mind and body? While burnout is not considered a medical diagnosis, the impact of burnout can lead to severe medical conditions, including high blood pressure, depression, heart disease, strokes, and more. Remember the statistics I shared in Chapter 2 highlighting the cost of healthcare due to destructive energy? There is a direct correlation between stress and health! Magnify these stories by tens or hundreds or thousands of employees and you realize that the health of organizations operating under level one energy is debilitating.

How incapacitating is this energy to organizations worldwide? "A new study by Asana[5] looked at over 10,000 knowledge workers across seven countries, and found approximately 70% of people experienced burnout in the last year."[6] How do these symptoms impact organizations? I'm sure every one of us can share stories for days on how this has personally impacted us and our organizations.

Deficient communication, poor collaboration, and low engagement are just a few symptoms companies experience daily under this energy level. What's even more concerning is that, because people are so withdrawn when in a state of level one energy, it becomes a company's silent killer. This is much different from its destructive counterpart, level two energy, which is consistently highlighted in the news. You will learn more about that in the next chapter.

Action Steps and Takeaways

Imposter Syndrome

Which types of imposters do you identify with?

1. **The Perfectionist:** Do you feel like your work must be 100% perfect, 100% of the time?
2. **The Superhuman:** Do you continue to constantly work after hours, even when you don't need to?
3. **The Natural Genius:** Are you used to "being the best" without expending too much effort?
4. **The Soloist:** Do you avoid collaboration or working in groups, as you know "you can get the job done on your own"?
5. **The Expert:** Are you constantly seeking out trainings or certifications because you think you need to improve your skills to succeed?

Limiting Beliefs
- What stories are your inner critics/gremlins telling you?
- What actually happened, and where did your imagination get creative?

- How can you separate fact from fiction to prevent these inner critics/gremlins from controlling your narrative?
- What shields have you built to keep yourself safe?
- How are those shields serving you?

Burnout

- Are you experiencing stress, or are you burned out?
- If you are experiencing burnout, how is this impacting your personal and professional life?
- What actions can you take to recharge your battery to prevent or diminish burnout?

Final Thoughts

What is the most important key takeaway from the Safety Zone? When you lose your ability to choose who you are and how you think, feel, and act, you empower a plot that was either given to you or impressed upon you. How can you take back your control? Here are five action steps you can take now to start shifting your storyline. As we continue to explore higher levels of energy, I will share five energetic success principles you can leverage to develop sustainable shifts, empowering you to design your own narrative as compared to the story from your inner critic.

Five Action Steps to Start Shifting Your Energy out of the Safety Zone

1. **Know Your Values:** When you know your values and have taken the time to uncover what matters to you the most and define it in your own words, you will have a surge of clarity in defining your life's mission and creating actions to drive

you towards accomplishing your goals. Do you struggle with saying no to offerings that don't serve you or that exhaust you? Here's a trick: only say yes to what aligns with your values! Visit this site to access my Values-Driven Solution Assessment.[7]

2. **Identify Your Inner Critic:** By identifying your inner critic, you will learn to thank these voices for trying to keep you safe and feel confident to let them know you're comfortable owning your worth and moving forward towards your goals.

3. **Separate Fact from Fiction:** When you look at what actually occurred versus the story you created, you empower the reality you want to find versus the story you've fabricated.

4. **Solicit Feedback:** Not sure how you present to others around you? Solicit feedback to see if your perception of yourself aligns with your family, friends, and colleagues.

5. **Celebrate Your Success:** Each of the five types of imposters focuses on failure and fear. One way to counter this is by changing your attitude to focus more on successes—no matter how small or big the accomplishment.

CHAPTER

5

The Combative Zone

Ladies and gentlemen, welcome to the main event! In this corner, weighing in at 222 pounds, is the heavyweight champion "News Editor." And in the other corner, weighing in at 215 pounds, is two-time undisputed division world champion, "Editor-in-Chief (EIC)." Gloves up, boxers! Let's get this match started!

Look at that! EIC is having a field day, just laying into News Editor, giving them a right royal boxing lesson. Each time News Editor tries to jab EIC, EIC flawlessly slips and rolls. Ouch! Look at that uppercut from EIC. I wouldn't be surprised if they knock out News Editor in this third round. One, two, three . . . oh, my goodness, News Editor is getting up! I can't believe it! How can they sustain this beating? Wait for it—do we see News Editor coming back?

Looks like News Editor is going to play dirty and throw some rabbit punches. We know that's illegal, but how can we blame them? They have taken beating after beating from EIC. Here we go, something new, we have some clinching . . . let's hope we don't have a Mike Tyson–Evander Holyfield situation on our hands. Ahh, EIC just landed a technical knockout (TKO). News Editor is officially terminated! What a bloodbath!

Combative Zone Qualities: Opposition, Frustration, Disobedience

Welcome to the tantalizing and aggressive level two energy, the most predominant energy people experience both at work and in their personal life. Level two energy is the second-lowest energy level, and, like all levels of energy, there are advantages and disadvantages to the zone. The core thought while approaching a situation with level two energy is judgment and conflict. People in a stressful state often feel angry, causing their reaction to be competitive and even combative.

The advantage of level two energy is its ferocious power, stemming from the amygdala. If you are faced with a threatening situation, level two energy can be used to fight versus flight or freeze. This is different from what we saw with level one energy. Why? Remember your cheat sheet from Chapter 3, the Energetic Self- Perception Wheel? In reviewing that, recall that each rising level of energy grows stronger away from self. Level two starts moving your energy outwards. Rather than blaming yourself for shortcomings, you start to defend yourself and project your frustration away onto external forces.

How can projecting outwards be an advantage? For those who default and suffer from level one energy, level two energy can become your gateway to using your voice. Rather than holding onto your aggravations internally, you can start to address what's really bothering you. On an individual level, I encourage my coaching clients to initially get a bit "spicier" to shift them from leading with level one energy to level two when they are experiencing a conflict. Here are a few tools you can use to take advantage of level two energy, using your voice to project outwards rather than internalizing your anger.

Direct Authentic Feedback

Direct authentic feedback enables you to communicate honestly, expressing what thoughts and emotions you're experiencing. If you are in an argument with someone or under severe stress, direct authentic communication empowers you to vocalize what is causing you friction.

- "I'm angry. I don't want to talk to you right now."
- "Parents, I will choose my career path. I'm not looking for your advice."
- "Colleague, I have a deadline of 5 p.m. Leave me alone so I can finish my work on time."
- "You are one of the smartest people I know, but saying 'um' so much makes you sound stupid."

When you read through each bullet point, what thoughts come to mind? Kim Scott, author of *Radical Candor*, shared the last bullet in reference to feedback she received from Sheryl Sandberg shortly after joining Google. Scott outlines the positive impact of this form of communication, which she defines as "Radical Candor," providing feedback that you "care personally and challenge directly."[1]

When you reflect on feedback you have received, how has this direct authentic approach made you feel? Are you cringing a little because it comes off a bit too blunt, and even curt? That concern is reasonable, and important to point out. This form of communication does not resonate with everyone.

Are you smirking at those you feel are too sensitive, thankful I finally pointed out the effectiveness of this form of communication under stress? That feeling is also understandable. Direct authentic feedback can be very efficient. Wherever you lie within the spectrum, we can all agree that the message being communicated using direct authentic feedback is clear. Depending on the pressure of the situation, it also might be the best form of communication to get the job done.

Call In and Calling Out

Commercial Archeologist: Rebe, move on out of that trench. You have been working on that all day and found nothing. I know you don't want to dirty up those girlie hands of yours, but you're never going to find anything until you learn how to manhandle a pit.

Commercial Archeologist Intern Rebe, Call-In Response: What was your intention with that comment?"

Commercial Archologist Intern Rebe, Call-Out Response: Your comment was unprofessional and sexist. Do not speak to me that way.

How would you classify Rebe's reaction to her leader's remark? She's probably furious! How does she vocalize her anger? By calling in or calling out her leader's critique. One response to conflict is the ability to use the call-in method, providing the wrongdoer an opportunity to reflect. You might remember your parents doing this as you were growing up. I can still recall my mom's voice when she was furious: "How do you think your actions impact the rest of your family?" The victim, Rebe, voices her frustration in the form of a question to offer the wrongdoer an opportunity to explore the impact of their comment or action, with the hope that their response results in a change in the wrongdoer's behavior moving forward.

The call-out method also empowers the victim to express their frustrations, but this method explicitly tells a person that their comment was unacceptable and will not be tolerated. This method is essential to immediately prevent a wrongdoer from causing more harm. You will see this technique explained and practiced in your workplace sexual harassment and violence training sessions. It's direct and effective to immediately stop a toxic situation from continuing.

Disciplinary Communication

Coming from over a decade in people services, I recommend disciplinary communication as a last resort to effectively correct an adult's behavior. I call out "adult" because, as we grow from being a toddler to adulthood, we all experience various forms of disciplinary actions from our parents and authority figures to learn about responsibility, safety, and the consequences of our actions.

Disciplinary communication in the workplace is used to modify an employee's unacceptable behavior or performance. Traditionally, this form of communication is used if an employee breaks a company policy, if coaching or performance management does not result in changed behavior, or if a corrective process is outlined in a collective bargaining agreement (CBA), which is a legal contract between an employer and an employee's representing union.

In general, we see disciplinary communication used on a progressive scale, allocating points to each infraction. Many of you might be familiar with time and attendance policies as an example. If an employee reaches a certain number of points, they are suspended, and later separated from an organization with just cause. "A 'just cause' dismissal (also referred to as 'dismissal for cause' or 'summary dismissal') is the termination of employment initiated by the employer in response to employee misconduct that is so serious that it either:

- Violates an essential condition of the employment contract.

- Breaches the trust or faith inherent in the working relationship.

- Is fundamentally or directly inconsistent with the employee's obligations to the employer."[2]

Delegation Orders

Delegation orders under conflict are effective and necessary to remove a threat or ensure a person's safety. Military and law enforcement consistently use this form of communication. "Watch your crossfire. Eliminate the threat." While the terminology is usually specific to its industry, the style is the same. The messaging is clear and ensures each person knows their responsibility, holding an individual accountable for their actions.

As you can see, the benefits of leading with level two energy to communicate your frustration ensures your message is expelled versus internalized. How else can level two energy be used to your advantage? Many even brag about how they work best under pressure. Stress becomes the perfect catalyst to "light a fire" under someone, ensuring they push through to the finish line.

While we see this can be true for specific situations, operating under continuous stress is not sustainable. The examples provided earlier in this chapter all showcase the power of level two energy in time-sensitive situations. The burst of energy that level two can provide ensures you can power through in that moment, or for that immediate need. The question becomes this: how long and how effectively can you run through quicksand?

The answer is, not very long. We are seeing the repercussions of this extended fury unfold more and more every day. How so? Each year, we continue to set new world records. We see these announcements all the time. Articles highlighting a company's success note that they've reached their "highest revenue" and "record-breaking sales." Internally, organizations also feature their accomplishments celebrating their "hardest worker" and "cost-savings strategies." While these metrics are an essential part of business, we aren't presenting the entire picture.

At what cost are our record achievements impacting the people who work to attain this recognition? Our world-record-success metrics have also come with an entire new set of breaking points exacerbated by the pandemic, leading to record-breaking mental health metrics. "Nearly one billion people worldwide suffer from some form of mental disorder, according to latest UN data—a staggering figure that is even more worrying, if you consider that it includes around one in seven teenagers."[3] The fire that was initially used to ignite people's motivation has turned into a wildfire of destruction.

So why is level two energy so pervasive, even though we know its destructive energetic impact? First, in addition to the amygdala's safety sensor, triggering a fight response with level two energy, scientists have found that negativity is cunning! It mirrors sensations such as joy and pride, falsely activating your brain's reward center. Consequently, this causes you to actually feel temporarily good when you indulge in negative emotions.

Second, our brains cannot process as much information as we have readily available. Around 11 million pieces of information are thrown at you at any given time, yet your brain can only process about 40 of those pieces.[4] To compensate, your brain creates mental shortcuts. The advantage of these mental shortcuts is that you can process information quickly when needed. The downside is these mental shortcuts are not reliable.

Daniel Kahneman, author of *Thinking, Fast and Slow*, explains why we create these mental shortcuts, categorizing the brain into two operating systems. System 1 is fast, processes 98% of your thinking, and the majority of what you process within this system is unconscious. System 2 is slow and is used to consciously processes the remaining 2% of the information thrown at you. System 2 comes into play largely when System 1 runs into a trying challenge. This is why you slow down and take time to process to make a decision when something difficult comes your way.

As you experience more pressure, with less time to process, your brain continuously resorts to System 1 to make decisions. While System 1 is fast, it has developed its catalogue of information based on your own experiences, rather than from a 360-degree lens. What's wrong with relying on this one perspective? It's biased and flawed! Whether you learned about optical illusions and perspectives in childhood through the Müller-Lyer Illusion, or from your family or community with the glass half full/half empty example, we all know there are multiple sides to any one story.

How does your brain's operating system impact your energy? When you're not "under fire," it's easier to leverage System 2 to question System 1, allowing you the time to question your initial thoughts and emotions, as well as look at a situation from a different perspective. Time gives you the opportunity to think, feel, and choose your response. Unfortunately, when you're constantly under stress, pressed for time, and literally trying to process a million things a minute, you get aggravated and react.

When you're angry and rushed, you're not even consciously making decisions—so much so that, many times, you don't even have control of your actions. Have you ever gotten so deep into an argument that you forgot how it started? Have you ever been so angry that your vision becomes cloudy? This is level two energy taking charge, which is why we sometimes say, "My emotions got the best of me." So how does this combative energy impact the workplace? Level two energy has taken control, perpetuating bias, communication deficiencies, discrimination, harassment, and even workplace violence.

Bias

When you think of a bias, what comes to mind? You're right, you have a bias against bias! A bias is a predisposition or affinity for or against a person or an object. We all have them, and there's nothing wrong with having some of them. Most times, you execute your preferences throughout the day, consciously and unconsciously, and don't pay any specific attention to your preferences or decisions.

So why are there so many negative connotations around the word bias? Please return to your Energetic Self-Perception Wheel in Chapter 3 and refer to the three columns. One column showcases thoughts, the second column depicts emotions, and the third lists actions. How do these three columns tie into bias? A bias holds no power when it's a *thought* that you acknowledge and question. A bias can impact your own energy, as it can *feel* gratifying or troubling. As soon as you *activate* your bias's thoughts and emotions against another person, your bias becomes destructive.

Explicit bias occurs when a person is purposefully partial or disapproving towards a person or group, perpetuating unfair treatment and inequality. Most people exhibit unconscious bias; 98% of their preference or aversion is not intentional. It's important to note that although 98% of your biases are unconscious, exercising this unconscious bias has detrimental effects on the workplace. Where do we see bias exhibited the most in the workplace? Bias has the most influence on whether or not certain candidates are hired. These biases can be seen before a candidate is even hired, throughout the talent acquisition (TA) process, in job descriptions, assessments, and interviews. Let's look at a variety of examples throughout the TA process and pull out where each bias exists and its destructive energetic impact.

Job Descriptions

T-Mobile, a US-based telecommunications company, prides itself on their culture and benefits. Their careers page highlights how "passion meets purpose" and that their differentiator is their people. As part of their DNA, they emphasize their commitment to diversity: "Be yourself. We like it that way. Diversity fuels our Un-carrier spirit. We're proud that diversity, equity, and inclusion are deeply embedded in all we do—from hiring and career development, to our award-winning culture."[5]

To ensure that their job descriptions (JDs) aligned with their value of diversity, T-Mobile hired Textio, an "advanced workplace language guidance, so you can see where social bias is hiding—and know exactly how to fix it."[6] Textio's software identifies bias in job descriptions, calling out terms that are exclusive to diverse groups. Examples include references to "he" or "she," excluding gender nonbinary candidates. Descriptors such as "go-getter" and "powerhouse" tend to be perceived as masculine terms, deterring women from applying. These descriptors also lack clarity and leave room for interpretation, not only with the candidate but also the hiring manager, increasing room for personal judgments and speculation. Experiences such as "graduate from a top university" and "digital native" display a potential bias based on age or socioeconomic stature. By following Textio's bias detection recommendations, T-Mobile saw a 17%

increase in female applications. When their JDs scored 90 or higher for bias-free language, they saw a five-day faster time to fill an opening on average.[7]

Assessments

Does your company use skill assessments to evaluate a candidate's ability to fill a role? If so, hiring managers must ensure that the assessment provided directly correlates with the needs of the role. While conducting a DEIA audit for a major cruise line in the travel and tourism industry, I quickly identified that a written skills test was being used to eliminate candidates who spoke English as their second language. However, English as their first language was not a requirement of the role. In fact, many of their roles required English as a Second Language (ESL), in conflict with this disqualifier. If a hiring manager is going to use a skills assessment to evaluate candidates, they need to ensure the testing skill directly aligns with the requirements of the job to eliminate this destructive bias.

Does your company use a behavioral assessment to evaluate if a candidate is a fit for your company's culture? Behavioral assessments such as the HBDI® (Herrmann Brain Dominance Instrument), the MBTI® (Myers-Briggs Type Indicator), or the AVA® (Activity Vector Analysis) provide data to assist recruiters and hiring managers with questions to learn more about a candidate's behavioral characteristics in the workplace. In conducting an audit on the use of AVA, in partnership with their leadership team, the AVA clearly demonstrated its validity, accuracy, and utility. However, its use within organizations shed light on discriminatory practices. Behavioral assessments, including the AVA, are meant to be used as tools to assist recruiters and hiring managers to ask questions to better understand a candidate's behavior. Companies who select random scores and use them as disqualifiers to eliminate candidates are using the tool incorrectly. This incorrect usage leaves these organizations open to unlawful business practices, discrimination, and legal implications.

Interviews

When you look at your interview evaluation process, how do your interview evaluation forms outline and define the purpose of each question, as well as each score? Do all questions directly tie back to your company values, key competencies, or requirements needed for the job? In reviewing the sample interview evaluation form shown in Figure 5.1, evaluate the quality of each question. How many questions leave room for interpretation?

Internship Interview Evaluation Form

Student Name: Referred By:

Interviewer: Date:

	Excellent	Good	Average	Below Average	Points Earned
Applicant's Greeting:					
• Proper introduction	10 9	8 7	6 5 4	3 2 1	
• Positive first impression	10 9	8 7	6 5 4	3 2 1	
Applicant's Appearance:					
• Neat, well groomed	10 9	8 7	6 5 4	3 2 1	
• Appropriately attired	10 9	8 7	6 5 4	3 2 1	
Personality and Poise:					
• Positive, courteous, sincere, and confident	10 9	8 7	6 5 4	3 2 1	
• Good posture, gestures, and eye contact	10 9	8 7	6 5 4	3 2 1	

FIGURE 5.1 Sample Interview Evaluation Form

Source: https://www.sampletemplates.com/business-/templates/interview-evaluation-form.html / Sample Templates

FIGURE 5.1 (Continued)

	Excellent	Good	Average	Below Average	Points Earned
Communication Skills:					
• Proper grammar (standard English)	10 9	8 7	6 5 4	3 2 1	
• Good pronunciation and enunciation	10 9	8 7	6 5 4	3 2 1	
• Pleasant voice and tone	10 9	8 7	6 5 4	3 2 1	
Responses:					
• Responded with appropriate answers	10 9	8 7	6 5 4	3 2 1	
• Showed knowledge of program's purpose	10 9	8 7	6 5 4	3 2 1	
• Indicated knowledge of Hospital	10 9	8 7	6 5 4	3 2 1	
• Asked appropriate questions	10 9	8 7	6 5 4	3 2 1	
• Volunteered information	10 9	8 7	6 5 4	3 2 1	
• Demonstrated initiative and enthusiasm about involvement in program	10 9	8 7	6 5 4	3 2 1	
Skills:					
• Showed evidence of career preparation	10 9	8 7	6 5 4	3 2 1	
• Showed evidence of good work habits	10 9	8 7	6 5 4	3 2 1	
• Showed evidence of problem-solving abilities	10 9	8 7	6 5 4	3 2 1	
Close of Interview:					
• Expressed a thank you	10 9	8 7	6 5 4	3 2 1	
• Concluded interview effectively	10 9	8 7	6 5 4	3 2 1	

Almost every single question! As a participant in this exercise, ask yourself, how many of these questions showcase how *you* feel? Almost every single question! If the candidate grew up in your same neighborhood, or you went to the same school, it's easy to see how you would rank them higher than if they grew up across the country and had a different background from you. Additionally, the scorecard does not define how to use the 1 to 10 rating system, leaving each score up to the interpretation of the interviewer.

Feelings you experience during an interview based on your own intersectional identities are not predictive of a candidate's success in completing their job. Your feelings are emotionally driven by your own personal perspective. When you use these feelings to qualify and disqualify candidates, your actions have a negative impact on the success of your team and organization. Why is empowering these biases so destructive? Let's look at five pervasive biases and their energetic impact to the workplace.

Affinity Bias

Affinity bias has dominated hiring decisions throughout our workplace, showcased in our DEI metrics. Entire organizations look and sound the same when leaders hire from a lens of affinity bias. How has affinity bias impacted our workplace makeup? As of May 2022, there were still only six Black CEOs on the Fortune 500 List, 20 Latinx CEOs, and only 8.8% of the Fortune 500 companies were run by women.[8] Even though organizations across the globe have recently prioritized talent acquisition and talent management with DEI initiatives to include trainings, interview guides, and scorecards, the workplace has a long way to go in highlighting this bias and correcting its destructive nature on our workplace's blueprint.

Gender Bias

The maternal wall is one of the most powerful destructive gender biases we see in the workplace. This bias typecasts mothers as being incompetent to work or focus their energy on anything outside of motherhood. The gender bias learning project reported that "compared to women with identical resumes but no children, mothers were:

- 79% less likely to be hired
- 100% less likely to be promoted
- Offered $11,000 less in salary for the same position
- Held to higher performance and punctuality standards"[9]

The Actor-Observer Bias

The actor-observer bias occurs when you have a propensity to accredit your actions to external factors, yet you attribute other people's actions to internal features. For instance, if you are running late to a meeting, you might blame traffic or an accident. However, if someone else is late to the same meeting, rather than attributing their tardiness to the same external dynamics that impacted you, you blame their tardiness on the fact that they're disorganized or slow. Have you ever been held to a different standard than someone else on your team? How did that make you feel? The actor-observer bias is a catalyst for unfair labor practices and discrimination claims worldwide.

Anchoring Bias

Have you ever been asked how much you made at your last job? If you've been paid below market and an employer or hiring manager continues to use your past salary as an anchor for your new pay, you've experienced anchoring bias. This one piece of information is used to anchor you or others around that source. How prolific is anchoring bias within compensation? In 2022, women still earned only $0.82 cents for every $1 earned by a man.[10] If you add up the difference in compensation year over year, by 65 years old, women are hundreds of thousands of dollars behind men.

Confirmation Bias

Confirmation bias has become the most impactful bias at present. No matter what your politics affiliation is, everyone knows the term "fake news." Confirmation bias confirms your beliefs by providing evidence to only support your thoughts, not to question them. Artificial intelligence has become so accurate that it leverages confirmation bias to reinforce our biases by selecting what news and advertising we're exposed to. This cycle has people more polarized in their personal and professional life than ever before, making it even more challenging for everyone to step into another person's shoes to learn about the world through their lens.

These biases and statistics are just a handful among hundreds that impact your thoughts every day. Take these cases as an opportunity to grow and learn about your own biases. The first step in shifting your energy, especially in a stressful situation, is to recognize them as they arise. By acknowledging them as they enter, you can then start to question their origins, creating shifts in your energy and negative impact to others.

Communication Deficiencies

Communication deficiencies are the gateway drug to perpetuating bias and are usually the first signs we see of someone exercising their bias inside the workplace. Like negative energy, communication deficiencies can be cunning. Let's look at a workplace investigation I conducted in 2019 and draw attention to each communication deficiency and its energetic impact.

In 2019, I received a call from a major US automotive company about a Hotline complaint they received, in tandem with multiple resignations from one of their stores. Their general counsel and GM believed it would be best for an outside consultant to conduct the investigation, because the leader in question had been with the organization for over 20 years and was not only one of their highest performers but was considered family.

As with all investigations, I reviewed details from the Hotline submission and conducted interviews with various employees to better understand the validity of the concern in question. In this investigation, the person who made the Hotline submission chose to remain anonymous. Additionally, they explained that they weren't 100% sure what they had witnessed. They noted that they wanted to raise the matter with leadership in case there was something problematic to address.

The person who wrote the Hotline—let's call them the witness—noted that they entered the executive offices after hours to obtain a printout, because their floor's printer was not presently functioning. While obtaining their printouts, they heard banging from the office of the VP of sales against the office of the director of sales. Additionally, they believed they heard discriminatory name calling coming from the office of the VP of sales. The witness identified the names on both offices but couldn't confirm who was in each office. They also confirmed that they did not hear anyone respond to the alarming name calling.

Within days of receiving the Hotline complaint, the director of sales and the sales manager both resigned from their roles, providing two weeks' notice. Both said they were moving to new cities, spoke highly of leadership, and wished everyone success on their continued journey with the organization. When HR reached out to conduct their exit interviews, conflicting information arose that caused them concerns to investigate further.

In the exit interview with the sales manager, she revealed that she consistently felt undermined by her VP of sales, but she was fearful of retaliation. She explained that her experiences were slight, and most people probably didn't even notice them. She highlighted multiple examples of microaggressions she experienced from being openly gay, and how those snubs impacted her productivity and engagement at work.

In connecting with the sales manager, I assured her that I understood what microaggressions are, and their impact on the energy of an individual and a team. Microaggressions can range on a spectrum from being intentional to unintentional against a marginalized population. There are three subgroups within microaggressions: microassaults, microinsults, and microvalidations. These communication deficiencies can be verbal, nonverbal, an action, and even environmental. Have you ever assumed someone's gender based on their name or position? Does your organization have grooming policies that exclude various hairstyles? Did you know that even certain soap dispenser sensors don't function for darker skin tones? These "slight" infractions perpetuate bias and directly correlate to the negative well-being of individuals, teams, and entire organizations.

Upon feeling heard, the sales manager continued to divulge she also suffered from being "heapeated" constantly and was tired of not getting recognized. *Hepeat* hasn't officially made it into the dictionary yet; however, the concept has presented a workplace struggle for years. Originally deriving from mansplaining, hepeat happens when a woman shares an idea and is not recognized for her contribution. However, if a man provides the same recommendation, he receives praise, without any acknowledgment that the idea had already been presented by a woman.

Upon completion of the sales manager's exit interview and statement, I reached out to the director of sales to complete his exit interview, as well as inquire about the matters that were brought forward in the Hotline complaint. My meeting with the director of sales commenced as a standard exit interview. He kept his answers very short and consistent. He was excited about a new opportunity across the country and was thankful for the mentorship his leader provided. Subsequently, I brought up the Hotline observation, explaining that there was a question about what occurred after hours one evening within the past few weeks. Did the VP of sales bang and yell discriminatory comments at the director of sales through their adjoining wall?

The director of sales looked me right in the eyes and said, "It's crazy, right?" He himself was questioning his understanding of events. He recounted numerous experiences where the VP of sales would bang on his door after hours and yell obscenities, but the concerns expressed by the director of sales were dismissed. He was told he was being sensitive, the bangs and yells weren't directed at him, or that his office just happened to be next door, so it seemed like he was in the "line of fire." The VP of sales went to far as to explain that the director of sales probably didn't understand his "drive" and "hunger" because no one else seemed alarmed about his demeanor. In fact, most found it motivating, a cultural addition to working in the US compared to APAC (Asia-Pacific).

After interviewing a handful of other team members in addition the VP of sales, I closed out the investigation and was able to circle back with the director of sales to validate his apprehensions. He wasn't going crazy; he was being gaslighted.

Gaslighting occurs when a person uses psychological methods to either make light of your emotions, or completely change the narrative of an event, so much so that you question your own understanding and sanity. Cases mirroring this example have become more prevalent, coming from management's responses to those calling in or calling out inappropriate behavior. Rather than focusing on the perpetrator or acknowledging the impact of their own actions, the victim is deemed overly sensitive or extremely emotional, further perpetuating a culture that is not psychologically safe.

How many communication deficiencies did you identify in reviewing this investigation? What biases were put into action that led to these deficits? How far did these transgressions spread from their original source? The detriment of this leader's short fuse impacted his direct reports, his team, his department, and the whole organization. Thankfully, the benefit of its combustion led to a recourse on psychological safety.

"Psychological safety is the belief that your environment is safe for interpersonal risk-taking."[11] In a psychologically safe workplace, people feel appreciated for their similarities and differences and feel empowered to bring their distinctive competencies to the forefront as a benefit to their team and organization. In this ideal workplace culture, every person prioritizes their time and energy to ensure their interactions build safety, share vulnerability, and establish purpose. This is what Daniel Coyle defines in his bestselling business book as the "Culture Code."[12] The opposite of the culture code is level two energy, where people have built barriers versus bridges, assumptions and judgments supersede vulnerability, and the collective purpose is *I or me* versus *us or we*.

Discrimination, Harassment, Violence

When trust is broken and an individual, team, or company is heavily operating from level two energy, the energetic impact is catastrophic! The majority of companies do not report on workplace violence on a large scale, in order not to add fuel to the fire of an already rampant blaze of negative energy. However, the statistics are hard to ignore.

Heading into 2023, two million Americans have declared that they have been a victim of workplace violence in the past year, with over 50% of cases coming from the medical industry. Nearly 30,000 women have reported cases of sexual assault in the workplace, and workplace bullying is at a record high number of 60.4 million infractions.[13] It's time to put our boxing gloves down. The pathway to destruction is imminent if we continue to work as if we're competing in a ring of fire. There is no final winner; we all lose. So how do we move forward and create a road of transformation?

The great news is that you don't have to continue living and working in destructive energy. In the upcoming chapters, we are going to cross over to constructive energy and start leveraging five energetic success principles to shift your energy from negative to positive.

Key Thoughts and Takeaways

1. What communication tools can you leverage with level two energy to express your frustrations rather than internalize your anger?
   - Direct authentic feedback
   - Calling in and calling out
   - Disciplinary communication
   - Delegation orders

2. Why do we create mental shortcuts, and why do these mental shortcuts results in bias?
   - Our amygdala signals us to detect "danger" when something is different from what we are used to, triggering level one energy (flight and freeze) as well as level two energy (fight). #nature

- We have millions of pieces of information coming at us at any given moment, yet we can only process about 40 pieces of information at a time.
- Mental shortcuts allow us to make decisions quickly, but unfortunately 98% of our decision-making is unconscious, based on our own experiences and perceptions. When we make quick decisions without questioning others' perspectives, we lead with our own biases. #nurture

3. What are biases?
   - A bias is a predisposition or affinity for or against a person or an object. We all have them.

4. When do biases become destructive?
   - When we put them into action against another person or situation.

5. I provided five examples of biases in the workplace and how they impact our workplace culture. What other biases can you identify in your workplace, and what is their energetic impact? (List any communication deficiencies that directly correlate to each bias, as well as any statistics that shed light on how prevalent each bias impacts your organization.)

Bias 1:

_____

_____

Bias 2:

_____

_____

Bias 3:

_____

_____

Looking for ways to disrupt your bias? Here are four steps you can take to start mitigating your bias:

Step 1: Evaluate your thoughts, emotions, and actions and take ownership of where you currently stand. By authentically honoring your current biases, you can create an action plan to mitigate their usage in your personal and professional life.

Step 2: Question what's coming up for you? Why are you having these thoughts? Why are certain emotions coming into play?

Step 3: Take a standing count of eight and breathe. You get to be your own referee anytime you want. Taking those eight seconds to pause before speaking or acting can shift your momentum. This leverages your ability to switch from System 1 to System 2 thinking, which provides you the opportunity to exercise choice versus reaction.

Step 4: Start to explore ways you can sustainably mitigate your bias. These eye-opening activities can be fun! Suggestions include:

- Attend a new cultural event, travel, listen to new music, read, and try new foods.

- If you are a hiring manager, ask your HR department how you can review resumes without the names.

- Jot down your stereotypes and journal how many times they pop up in the day so you can form new associations and diminish those judgments.

- Connect with someone who has an opposing view to yours and ask them to walk you through their story.

These activities will ultimately lead to what Dr. Janet B. Reid and Vincent R. Brown call "bias disruptors" in their book *Intrinsic Inclusion*:

- Shared trust
- Respectful empathy
- Connected understanding
- Significant emotional relationships

Final Thoughts

In the upcoming chapters, we will unearth how these four bias
disruptors are embedded into higher energy levels. For now, it's
most important for you to take this chapter's key takeaways and
action steps to ascertain how heavy level two energy weighs upon
your thoughts, emotions, and actions, and how this depletes your
own personal energy, as well as the energy of those around you.
Each time a stressor impacts your energy, call yourself out! How
quickly do you shift from "we" to "me," ensuring you "win" and
others "lose"?

CHAPTER

6

The Compromise Zone

Congratulations! You have officially made it to the bridge between destructive and constructive energy. As promised in Chapter 3, we had to commence with heavy lifting, identifying what is weighing you down and where you are operating under lower levels of energy. Now that you have pushed through the resistance of level one and level two energy, we will shift gears to a flat road. Understandably, after exerting all that energy to get up the hill, all you probably want to do is coast. Well, you have made it to exactly that point.

Level three energy is the conduit from destructive to constructive energy. This energy is very useful because it empowers people to focus on the positive versus the negative. Those who lead with level three energy are masters at reconciling difficult situations. They leverage their energy to align people and teams to motivate themselves and others to move forward. Ultimately, you can use this energy as an escape route from feeling defeated or angry, allowing you to see the positive side of a situation.

87

The drawback to level three energy is that many stay in this zone, believing that they're just "fine." When a person feels "fine," they tend to want to keep the "peace" and trade off on their wants and desires to avoid feeling stressed or fearful. When you consistently compromise on your wants and desires, you hold yourself back from attaining true happiness.

Compromise Zone Qualities: Accountability, Resilience, Compromise

I like to explain the three advantages and disadvantages of level three energy as yin and yang. On one side of the spectrum, those who lead with level three energy take responsibility for their actions. One of the drawbacks to responsibility is that you might be a poor delegator and micromanage your team. Stemming from responsibility, level three energy empowers people to be resilient. While resilience is key to ensuring you can bounce back from hardship, it's important to note when resilience can shift to persistence, stemming from anger and frustration (level two).

When stakeholders don't align and you must forge a path forward, something has to give. Compromising to achieve a shared goal is different from settling on a less than ideal solution. When we accept that a less than ideal situation is "fine," we forgo our passion to strive for higher levels of energy. Let's delve into these yin and yang relationships and see how they impact individuals, teams, and organizations.

The Compromise Zone Objectives

To better understand the objective of level three energy, let's return to your Energetic Self-Perception Wheel from Chapter 3. In reviewing the chart, you will see that level three energy is the first energy level to exit the ring of "self." How does this shift impact your perspective when experiencing this energy? As you recall, with level one energy you feel as if you're losing and have no control, blaming yourself for your shortcomings. When you experience level two energy, you blame others for how you feel and act, causing you to fight to ensure "you" win and "they" lose.

Level three energy is the first level of energy where you own your thoughts and feelings and take responsibility for yourself and your actions. Additionally, as ego continues to fade, for the first time you welcome others to join you in your success. But remember, this energy zone straddles both destructive and constructive energy. Even though you might invite others to join you in your success, you still make sure you win first—similar to how a host may love to wine and dine friends, but always sits at the head of the table.

Let's look at our first host of this chapter, a casting director and CEO of a well-known international casting agency. Early in January 2018, I received a call from Elizabeth, a successful casting director in London, who worked under the "host" (as described in the previous paragraph). Elizabeth said she was referred to me through mutual connections from my study abroad program in Cannes, where she also spent various summers learning French. She was seeking both coaching and consulting services, because she was ready to open her own casting agency and branch out from her current employer. She was clearly distraught when she called, exhibiting a mix of emotions from anger to relief, sadness to excitement.

In our initial call, I asked Elizabeth to walk me through her journey. Where did her story begin, and what led her to her current energetic state? Elizabeth explained that she had worked for the same casting agency for nine years. It had all started in 2011, within a few years after graduating from university. She had been working as a food server in Marylebone but knew she had a passion for film. She didn't know exactly which area of the entertainment industry she wanted to pursue, but she had strategically transferred to London from Brighton and hoped the universe would guide her to her destination.

That summer, she got her opportunity. One of her colleagues' roommates was a costume design intern and heard that one of the global casting agencies had an opening for an assistant. Knowing Elizabeth was looking for an in, she put in a good word to the team on set. Elizabeth jumped at the opportunity, interviewed for the role with the CEO, and was offered the assistant role on a trial basis.

Within her first week of work, a director hit on her, and offered her a "chance" to move offices, with an invitation to dinner. Rather than accepting, she politely declined, and disclosed the experience to her CEO. Her CEO applauded her courage and authenticity and offered her a full-time job on the spot. She promised Elizabeth she would have to work harder than she'd probably ever had to work before, but she would teach her how to be a successful casting director, as she was known in the industry as indisputably one of the best.

In her first few years of working under her CEO, Elizabeth was a sponge, working extensive hours as her boss's right hand. She witnessed how her CEO obtained new projects, selected and developed talent, negotiated contracts, and managed the various personalities who touched each film she cast. Elizabeth became a mirror reflection of her CEO. She mastered her taste and processes, and anticipated her boss's needs before she even asked. She worked 10–12 hours a day, including weekends at a time, to master these skills. She didn't have any time for a social life and justified surrendering her personal life to achieve success in her professional life. Her CEO echoed and encouraged her sentiment. She had built her business on her own. The dedication needed to succeed in casting meant sacrificing a partnership and family.

Actors' and directors' needs always came first. It's the way the business operates.

Elizabeth's loyalty to her CEO and commitment to her work paid off. In just over two years, she was promoted to casting associate, which came with her own office and projects. She was ecstatic to grow and was enthusiastic about providing her insights to the projects she was tasked to manage. Up until this point, every form of communication she created had to be approved by her CEO. Since each communication came directly from her boss's inbox, her boss took responsibility for ensuring each communication reflected her voice and direction. She also took responsibility for any mistakes or backlash from clients, which Elizabeth was very thankful for. The checks and balances system they set up allowed Elizabeth to learn without fear of repercussions from external sources.

In addition to Elizabeth's promotion, she was asked one request. Her CEO believed the support she provided was unmatched. Because the two worked so closely with each other for extensive hours, their professional relationship grew to a strong bond of trust that had developed over time, through vulnerable conversations about their goals, both personal and professional. Therefore, her CEO offered her the promotion with the caveat that she would have to play dual roles until she found and trained her a new assistant. Elizabeth felt responsible for ensuring the transition was smooth, as she was grateful for the dedication with which her CEO provided her in training and promoting her. She accepted the arrangement, assuming she would hire and train someone in the upcoming weeks.

After months of hiring and separating assistants that her CEO didn't "like," Elizabeth started to feel resentful and exhausted. It was apparent to her that her CEO didn't want anyone other than Elizabeth herself, which was holding her back from jumping into her new role. Additionally, she was still required to run all communication through her CEO, as her CEO still associated her with being her assistant, even though Elizabeth had her own projects.

Elizabeth finally gathered up enough courage and voiced her concerns. She even asked her boss, "Do you trust me? Do you have concerns about the quality of my work? Why did you promote me to a new role that you aren't allowing me to step into?" Her CEO listened intently and answered Elizabeth's questions. She admitted that she had a hard time relinquishing control, and validated Elizabeth's frustrations. She also applauded Elizabeth for having the courageous conversation with her about her sentiment. She commended Elizabeth for her outstanding work. Ultimately, she agreed to train her new assistant, the way she had trained Elizabeth, and would allow Elizabeth to move into her new role.

Over the next two years, Elizabeth continued to excel and take on bigger projects. She still ended up keeping some pieces of her assistant role, as her CEO never 100% felt comfortable offloading all responsibilities to anyone other than her. Elizabeth accepted those obligations and "just let it go." As a side note, she did tell me that her boss constantly gave her presents to thank her for her additional support. She acknowledged that she accepted the gifts as a thank-you for the assistant support she provided her, but really these gifts spoke personally to her love language.

During this period of her tenure, Elizabeth started recognizing the impact of still not having a social life. In connecting with others in her role outside of her office, each shared why they loved casting, specifically because of the flexibility it provided for both a personal and professional life. She started to realize the lack of work-life balance was much more about her CEO than the industry. She "tabled" that information at the time, with the hope that she would step into the "luxury" of a work-life balance after she became a casting director. For the most part, she was performing her role and continuing to learn every day. When she looked at her career in totality, she was thankful and proud of herself.

Once again, just around two years into her role as a casting associate, Elizabeth was recognized for her achievements and was promoted to casting director. Her growth came with additional responsibility, which included overseeing a team of associates. Elizabeth was also starting to get recognized within the industry. Her eye for diverse talent was unique. DEI hadn't been a priority within the industry, and Elizabeth was pioneering DEI efforts. Directors started reaching out to her CEO, specifically asking for Elizabeth to be the lead on projects.

As Elizabeth received more recognition, she noticed her boss's energy shifting towards her intermittently. For instance, when they were in meetings, she would purposely ask Elizabeth to bring her coffee in front of high-profile clients, highlighting that Elizabeth was her "best assistant" even though she had grown into a casting director role. She would also call out Elizabeth's insecurities in front of the team, passing them off as personal jokes between the two. Her cunning microaggressions were a not-so-subtle way of reminding her who was "boss."

Other times, she would pop champagne and amplify Elizabeth's success to the entire organization, attributing their "win" to her talents. The roller coaster of emotions was confusing, but Elizabeth didn't feel it was worth bringing up in conversation because she didn't want to provoke her boss in any way. Elizabeth complained to friends, family, and colleagues, but for the most part she loved her job, and she commended herself for being so resilient and continuing to excel in her career. To keep herself safe, she pulled back on all things personal in the office, closing off any vulnerable conversations that she used to engage in with her CEO and team. She also crafted a workaround for the assistant tasks her boss asked for, delegating them to her team, with the stipulation that everything come back through her, so it appeared that she performed the requests as asked.

As Elizabeth continued to build a name for herself within her organization, she started to explore ways in which she could enhance the company's business development. The office was very well known in London and had an international reputation. However, New York City was primarily an untapped market for them. Most actors in New York were Broadway performers who worked with local casting agencies. Elizabeth had a passion for New York City and looked at poaching this untapped market as an opportunity. Within weeks of her pursuits, which her CEO encouraged, she was bringing in new business. How do you think her CEO responded to the additional business and revenue?

If you are a CEO reading this at present, you're probably jumping with excitement. Many companies make individuals partners for bringing in business, expanding their reach, brand, and impact. Unfortunately, her CEO did not respond accordingly. Once again, she demonstrated typical level three interplay. At first she responded with anger. She was jealous, even though Elizabeth was someone she had invested in and developed to be exactly as she designed (level two). Upon reflecting on her jealousy, she started to doubt herself. Was Elizabeth a better casting director than she was? Was Elizabeth more likable than she was (level one)? Ultimately, she came to acceptance (level three).

The additional business Elizabeth brought in was a value-add for her and her organization. She acknowledged the vital role she played in coaching Elizabeth to the successful level she was performing at, as well as the success of her team. She met with Elizabeth, and congratulated her on her success and for bringing in business. She apologized for her initial reaction and shared more about her insecurities. Once more, the word "responsibility" came to the forefront. Her CEO looked at her organization like a family and felt it was her role to be the "mother hen," so much so that she viewed business development as her duty to ensure she supported her "family."

Yet again, Elizabeth accepted her apology, trying to give her CEO the benefit of the doubt. After all, she knew her boss had to fight to be a female leader in entertainment, a space traditionally run by men. However, she felt her energy draining. Each time she took strides forward in her career, she felt the boomerang effect from her CEO. She was tired of managing her boss's emotions. This is what led her to call me for an exploratory discussion.

Elizabeth planned on continuing to work under her CEO but wanted a plan of action to start separating ties. She knew she needed to fly under the radar, so she discontinued pursuing new business. She started to recommend others to take on the more demanding projects, and used the extra time she gained to network, conducting informational interviews, and build out a business plan for her own company. She quietly quit, giving only exactly what was required.

Within a year of us working together, Elizabeth gave her notice and partnered with a New York casting director, looking to expand their international reach. On her last day, everyone could feel the "pink elephant in the room" but no one wanted to address any real emotions. Nine years summed up to "thank you for your contributions, wishing you the best in your next adventure." Elizabeth felt a mix of emotions. She mourned the loss of her boss and team. At times she couldn't believe her once intimate relationship had turned so transactional and superficial. She was angry that her CEO's energy turned competitive against her. She was thankful for everything she learned. She was excited for her next adventure. Ultimately, she was going to be just fine.

In reviewing Elizabeth's story, where can you point out level three energy? Let's analyze each dualism and evaluate the energetic impact each has on individuals, teams, and organizations.

Accountability

Accountability is a key attribute of level three energy. Those who consistently lead with level three energy take responsibility for their actions and ensure they follow through on their commitments. They're dependable. Even when they make a mistake, they accept accountability for the role they played.

Organizations cannot function without this essential characteristic. Look at any interview evaluation forms. How many questions circle back to accountability?

- Tell me a time when you accomplished a goal and the steps you took to achieve your accomplishment.
- Tell me a time when you made a mistake at work.

It's imperative that everyone take ownership of the role they play in order for organizations to execute their mission and progress towards their goals. How can accountability be a disadvantage of level three energy? While those who lead with level three energy are reliable, at times the responsibility they regard may not be theirs to maintain. How so?

When leading with level three energy, it's easy to overstep and hijack someone else's duties as your own. How many times have you caught yourself managing someone else's task or job? When something isn't getting done in the time or way you would have handled it, many times we perceive it to be easier to jump in and just get it done. I have been guilty of doing this throughout my life!

How often do you catch yourself thinking or saying, "It's easier for me to just do it myself"? If you're the person leading with level three energy jumping in, it's hard to see how this negatively impacts those around you. However, if you are the person whose task or role just got seized, it's easy to understand how frustrating this feels. When you capture another's work as your own, you deprive them of their opportunity to grow. You are also communicating, whether consciously or unconsciously, that you don't trust them to complete their assignment.

What's ironic is that most people who acquire others' roles end up dipping into level one and level two energy, frustrated that they "had" to jump in and lead. Who asked you to jump in? No one—this is the story you're telling yourself. Unless asked, you did not "have" to undertake anything. The lesson for you is to step back and allow "the owner" to take accountability. Just because "the owner" isn't executing the same way you would doesn't mean their way is wrong.

In reviewing Elizabeth's experience, we see that her CEO took accountability for the work her organization put out. Her shortcoming was that responsibility became a control mechanism to micromanage her team. A micromanager's intent is to mitigate risk. However, the consequences of micromanaging stifles individuals from developing and decreases a team's energy due to inefficient processes and distrust.

Distrust plus inefficient processes results in poor customer service, both internally and externally. Not only does your organization lose money due to low morale, low productivity, and the resulting turnover, but you also lose business because of your team's impact on your end customer. In this case, Elizabeth even stopped bringing in business as a direct result of her CEO's reaction. Based on her current portfolio, her boss lost a revenue potential of $1 million annually.

Resilience

Level three energy empowers resilience, because this energy allows you to identify a path forward to recover from challenges. When you channel this energy, you proactively leverage the tools we've discussed to exit level one and level two energy. These tools include pausing to reflect, leading with curiosity to identify an opportunity, and reframing your perspective.

The American Psychological Association defines resilience as "the process and outcome of successfully adapting to difficult or challenging life experiences, especially through mental, emotional, and behavioral flexibility and adjustment to external and internal demands." As we learned with level one and level two energy, your brain is wired to identify risks and tries to keep you safe. Resilience becomes your lever to turn down level one and level two energy to ensure you can adapt to change.

When your culture and employees embody resilience, your workplace becomes flexible and buoyant. Dell Technologies, in partnership with the Institute for the Future (IFTF), estimate that 85% of the jobs that will exist in 2030 aren't even conceived yet![1] As the workplace continues to evolve at a rapid place, resilience becomes a key ingredient to ensuring your organization stays relevant and alive.

Throughout her nine-year journey, where did you see Elizabeth practice resilience? As an assistant, she reframed her relationship with being micromanaged as an opportunity to learn exactly what her boss wanted, so much so that she anticipated her needs. As she progressed into leadership roles, she practiced resilience, managing multiple positions, including training her predecessor. When her CEO continued to toggle between praising her and undermining her success with sarcastic remarks and slights, Elizabeth shifted her energy to perseverance, creating an action plan to become her own boss.

Unexpected challenges will always arise at work. However, as we saw with Elizabeth's story, resilience is required to survive in a toxic workplace environment. What had to give in order for Elizabeth to continue to push forward? When Elizabeth started working for her boss, she shared how vulnerable each was, creating a trust and psychologically safe environment. As her CEO's energy started to shift, she used Elizabeth's vulnerability against her, breaking their trust. How do you think this made Elizabeth feel? How much energy do you think Elizabeth expended exhibiting resilience to surge forward? How many ways could this energy have been put to better use?

If companies repurposed even a fraction of the resilient energy consumed by their employees to cope with inefficient processes, psychologically unsafe work environments, and toxic workplace practices, to creating a proactive and motivational workplace culture, who knows how much their employees could accomplish! In this example, if we took the cost of gifts given to Elizabeth divided by the number of unwarranted infractions, each task would equate to about $100/hour. The potential for possibility is incalculable.

Compromise

F***!
I can't. I can't believe this. I can't do this. I just can't.
No, it's not that bad. I'll figure it out.
Everything is going to be just fine.
Does this sound like your typical merry-go-round response when an unexpected challenge arises? Elizabeth laughed when I named this her daily mantra. I hear this cyclical response so much that I've made a TikTok dance to it. Since you've become an expert in identifying destructive energy, let's see if you can identify where it pops up in this modulation.

F*** is typical level two energy. A challenge just arose, which understandably makes you angry. I can't. I can't believe this. I can't do this. I just can't. Here comes level one with its self-doubt and fear, wanting you to avoid this feeling and retreat to safety. No, it's not that bad. I'll figure it out. Here is where you start to identify where you may be compromising and prioritizing what's most important. Everything is going to be just fine. Congratulations! The "N" and the "E" got you to level three energy. Rather than yielding to destructive energy, level three energy becomes the passage to positivity. No matter what, you are going to figure it out and be just fine.

How do you define the "fine"? Most define it as acceptable and satisfactory.

- How's work? "Fine."
- How's the family? "They're fine."
- How's your morning going? "Just fine."

Fine sits on the surface. It allows people to acknowledge their own and others' sentiments as adequate and reasonable enough to continue moving forward. What's wrong with that? Considering a person's typical day, most would say, nothing. The morning wakeup call comes with a preparation checklist. Somewhere within your 24-hour day, you're expected to be engaged and productive for about eight hours of work-work. Finally, the evening itinerary includes a list of follow-up items and activities before you're allowed to shut down and start all over.

When you exacerbate this breakdown with the intersectional identities that make up your life, it's understandable that many don't have more energy to strive for more. Which explains why so many people settle for level three energy. Compromising on passions and joy creates a safety net to ensure you don't experience more hardship and pain. We see this constantly in how people manage their relationships. For fear of getting hurt, they dim their desires.

How does this impact the workplace? Level one and level two energy have saturated the workforce. After companies finally settled into processes and procedures to manage the ever-changing challenges additionally brought forth from the pandemic, level three energy has also become a welcomed relief. Hence the trend of quiet quitting.

In alignment with level three energy, your view of quitting depends on your perspective. Studies show the average human is only productive three or four hours a day at work. Therefore, if everyone quietly quits on your team for the first time, you may rely on your employees to give exactly what is requested of them. When a person quietly quits, they can re-allocate their energy to their priorities. When they don't expend all their energy at work, a person can practice work-life balance, prioritize their wants and needs, and set boundaries to have energy in both their personal and professional lives. Why do people have a negative perception of quiet quitting?

Companies are constantly striving to engage their employees and have created an entire movement of defining their culture to connect their team members to their vision and mission. The more engaged your workforce, the stronger your competitive advantage. Passionate employees who strive to go "above and beyond" drive customer service, innovation, and productivity.

When we look at Elizabeth's storyline, how many times did she compromise on her wants and needs? She worked 10–12 hours to succeed at work, to make concessions in her personal life. She took on work that was no longer her responsibility, in fear of her boss's confrontational energy. Ultimately, Elizabeth succeeded in departing, but at what cost?

I like to compare leading with level three energy to putting glitter on garbage. On the surface, it looks fine. But if you don't address your fears, what's holding you back from living in alignment with your values to accomplish your goals, you'll never reach higher levels of energy to propel you forward. I don't make this statement out of judgment against level three energy. Remember, you have the power to choose which energy levels you want to leverage. When you're comfortable with something being fine, own your feelings. When you're ready to address what's under the glitzy glitter, honor the emotions that will come with that light switch. Similar to how we started off this book, you'll have to work through what's causing you pain before you can truly attain everything you have to gain.

Action Steps and Takeaways

1. When do you lead with level three energy, and how is this energy advantageous and disadvantageous in your workplace and life?

   _____

   _____

   _____

2. What are three key attributes within the Compromise Zone?

   1. Accountability

   2. Resilience

   3. Compromise

Accountability:

   1. How has taking ownership and accountability in your life improved your relationships in both your personal and professional life?

2. Do you identify any opportunities to release responsibility, as the task or role is not yours to own? If so, how has that impacted those around you?

Resilience:

1. Are you constantly exhibiting resilience to forge a path forward due to a toxic work environment?

2. How can you repurpose your energy, so you aren't having to constantly live in a state of resilience?

Compromise:

1. How do you balance compromising the team's individual goals to ensure the collective achieves its mission and purpose?

2. Identify opportunities in your life where you are settling for "fine"? Do you want to strive for more in any of these areas? What's holding you back from attaining your passions and goals? What possibilities could you achieve if you addressed where you are experiencing level one or level two energy?

Final Thoughts

The Compromise Zone is one of the most challenging energy zones to identify and shift. Those consistently experiencing level three energy take responsibility for their actions, and are master rationalizers of their thoughts, feelings, and actions. In this chapter, I highlight the shift from destructive to constructive energy, and where it serves and doesn't serve the reader. The key takeaways and action steps will allow you to evaluate where you're settling for feeling "fine," where you're avoiding feeling or addressing pain, and where they can feel more excited and energized to create any possibility you desire!

CHAPTER
7

The Service Zone

When was the last time you experienced amazing hospitality? Do you have a favorite restaurant, coffee shop, or bar where the server knows your order by memory? Is there a specific hotel or hotel brand you book each time that welcomes you back by name? Or maybe the local pediatrician took your call at 2:00 a.m., calming you in the middle of the night in a time of need and distress? How about the organization's HR department? Does a person stand out for spending that extra time with you to ensure the medical plan you chose met your family's wellness needs?

Whatever moment comes to mind, each of these hospitable experiences shares a common theme. They all leave you with a feeling, a sentiment that makes you feel special and comforted. This energy of warmth comes from the heart and is a beautiful gift that stems from level four energy, the service zone.

Service Zone Qualities: Hospitable, Caring, Problem-Solving, Empathetic

Individuals whose leading energy stems from the service zone focus their attention towards caring for others. In fact, those who lead with providing service gain energy when they can assist others around them, making this one of the most desirable energy levels for organizations to seek in their people. Why? Customer service expert Shep Hyken explains it best: "The one statistic that matters most is if the customer comes back."[1] When you experience something exceptional, these moments stand out, making you want to return. Each time you return and experience another favorable interaction, your brand loyalty increases.

Soon enough, the local coffee shop becomes *your* Starbucks. The Ritz Carlton becomes *your* family's second home. Dr. Guzamano becomes *your* pediatrician. Bethany becomes *your* go-to benefits guru. What do you do as soon as something becomes yours, or a person becomes part of your community? You start to care for it or them, making this gracious energy cyclical. Hospitable employees build repeat customers. Repeat customers drive revenue and stability. Stable revenue drives growth and innovation.

So why do we see the highest resignation rates across the US specifically coming from service-industry jobs? The drawback of caring for others before your own needs is that your caring energy can lead to burnout, frustration, self-doubt, and exhaustion. Throughout this chapter, I will demonstrate how individuals who lead with level four energy can sustain their compassion for others, but also remain energized. I will walk through examples where leading with empathy can be used to connect with others, but the energetic principle of detachment can also allow entities and teams to separate themselves from carrying other's energy as their own, as well as detach from their own personal solution.

Ultimately, I will exhibit how organizations can lead with level four energy to enhance their practices and procedures to foster an environment of care, an energy their employees will reciprocate full circle.

Service Zone Case Studies

Let me start by introducing you to Jasmine, a 35-year-old animated, curly-haired Boston native. If you asked Jasmine how she came into her role as a vice president of human resources (HR), she would tell you she knew from day one that she's always had a passion for people and loves helping those in need.

She's one of five siblings, so it was easy to get lost among the everyday drama and commotion of family. Throughout her childhood, emotions constantly ran high; voices rang even louder. To navigate, Jasmine learned her superpower quite early on. She became a "master of service." She loved being there for each family member when a challenge arose. She became their confidant and kindhearted listener, catering to their wants and needs, creating an ecosystem of stability amid the family chaos.

After years of practice, Jasmine's balancing act paid off, making it no surprise that she energetically jumped in and excelled at HR. After working seven years for a government contractor through talent acquisition, compensation, benefits, and HR operations, Jasmine was ready to expand her expertise to a senior leadership role. She accepted an offer to be the director of HR for a tech startup, specifically servicing the virtual event space.

Day one in her new role, Jasmine jumped onto Slack, of course, looking to see where she could be of assistance. She became well versed on processes and procedures. Jasmine valued forging meaningful relationships, so she took time to Zoom with every individual across the globe, ensuring that the organization's culture scaled as they expanded. She became the go-to for leaders companywide. Every time she met a new team member, her energy increased. Each time she solved a problem, her energy increased. Each time she was able to be a resource to enhance operations, her energy increased. So why, at the end of the day, was Jasmine so exhausted?

Jasmine is a classic example of how level four energy can both boost and deplete your energy. The genuine emotion she feels when caring for those around her is thoughtfulness and compassion. Her energy increases as she provides support and attention to the needs of those around her and prioritizes their well-being to ensure they love their roles as much as she loves hers. She's an expert in understanding her surroundings, observing, and listening, and many times, anticipating her coworkers' needs. She feels successful when she's able to help others with challenges and provide solutions, making her a great advisor and motivator at work and at home.

The challenge is that, because she prioritizes others first, many times her own needs get neglected. What happens when you give out all your energy but neglect refueling your own tank of energy? The service you provide, which naturally gives you excitement and joy, can quickly shift your perspective. Rather than feeling resourceful, you might start to feel used and depleted. Instead of enjoying helping others, you might start to think your help is a burden you wish you didn't have to provide. By the end of the day, you're frustrated, drained, and exhausted.

How can one who leads with level four energy stay energized to continue to do what they love most? By learning these three lessons:

- Lesson 1: Prioritize Your Energetic Needs
- Lesson 2: Empathize and Release
- Lesson 3: Detach from Your Solution

The next three sections explain each of these.

Lesson 1: Prioritize Your Energetic Needs

By March 2021, just three months into her new role, Jasmine started questioning her decision about accepting this director opportunity. She loved her work but was just worn out. She was trying to appease everyone yet was failing at satisfying anyone. When have you experienced this same sentiment, and how did it serve you? For Jasmine, she noticed herself missing deadlines, cutting corners, making small errors at first, and then larger ones that impacted the team members she valued so much. On top of that, Jasmine was also failing in her personal life. Her partner wanted more of her time and energy, but she had nothing to give by the time she got home. Friendships also started to dissipate, as her "yes" to every offer left her double-booked and split between family and friends.

There's only so much one can take on, before one's personal energy shuts down emotionally, physically, and mentally. The high of helping others becomes too much to take on, causing one's energy to deplete to lower levels of energy. The natural next response is to either get angry (level two) or succumb to exhaustion and avoid dealing with the situation (level one), both shutting you off from the rest of the world.

By the end of March 2021, Jasmine knew something needed to change. She missed loving her work and excelling in her career and life. The "hamster wheel" effect of feeling high at the beginning of the day and then crashing and burning at night, just to do it all over again, was not supporting her goals. She needed a sustainable solution to shift her energy. It was time to hire a leadership coach.

In working with me, Jasmine immediately identified how much energy she had at the beginning of the day. This realization led her to be curious. What caused her to be so energized in the morning, but depleted by noon?

When reviewing her schedule, Jasmine quickly acknowledged her morning priorities. Her top value is connecting with others, which means she loves spending time getting to know a person, communicating with them, and being present to their needs. Knowing how much energy and joy these interactions gave her, she prioritized her morning meeting with people, giving her something to look forward to when she started the day. She scheduled one-on-ones with her team, interviews for open roles, and coaching sessions with leaders.

The challenge was that Jasmine scheduled back-to-back 30-minute meetings, yet always went over by at least 15 minutes. Her value of having meaningful relations outweighed her need to keep organized and on schedule. How many times have you noticed time fly by when you're in a one-on-one or an interview with a candidate you love? It's natural to continue to explore your chemistry with a person, especially when in flow! (This is level six—more to come on this energy level later.)

Additionally, Jasmine quickly noticed that she didn't schedule any time between meetings to process, decompress, and prioritize her needs of self-care. Bristol Myers Squibb (BMS) has made it a company practice to schedule all meetings either 25 minutes or 50 minutes long to ensure their employees prioritize this down time before jumping into another activity. Five or ten minutes might do the trick, but it's important to ask yourself how much time you personally need to reflect and deliberate, especially on something as important as selecting a potential new team member.

The energy Jasmine gained from providing service to others became instantly depleted as soon as she got behind schedule. When someone who leads with level four energy feels rushed to provide quality service, their natural reaction leads to frustration (level two) or guilt (level one). By noon, Jasmine was spending more time sending out apologies and rescheduling meetings than holding the meetings and doing the work she loved. Most nights, her schedule shifted from ending at 5:00 p.m. to crashing at 8:00 p.m., and numerous times even bled into the next day. How often does this happen to you?

For our first shift, Jasmine updated her meetings to one hour long. The increased meeting time may seem excessive; however, this allowed her to prioritize her desire to spend time with others, which naturally enhanced her engagement and energy. She communicated the reason for the adjustment, sharing her passion for bonding with her team, interviewees, and colleagues, with the caveat that the whole time might not be needed. This easy change became a huge energetic shift.

Jasmine instantly noticed where she was cutting corners, depleting the quality of her work. She hadn't even realized how much she was leaning on assumptions and interpretations in her interviews, biases that were created strictly out of her need for more time! Unlocking this blind spot gave Jasmine an opportunity to shift her perspective. She started to look forward to her meetings even more now because she knew she had the time to get personal and be present. The energy she brought to the meeting also created an energetic shift in her counterparts, who could feel her excitement and care, allowing them the space to open more and be present, creating that cyclical constructive energetic cycle I highlighted earlier.

Second, Jasmine rearranged her schedule. After testing out a few different ways to organize her calendar, Jasmine found herself most energized when she could consistently switch from interacting with people to focusing on projects. Since interactions with people brought her the most energy, she spread them out as "treats" throughout her day. This may seem like a minimal change, but it became a huge change in Jasmine's outlook. Rather than looking at her morning as a marathon checklist, her calendar started to balance how her energy ebbed and flowed, providing her sustainable energy she could uphold during the course of her day.

The final adjustment Jasmine needed to make to her schedule was not only designing breaks but looking at how to maximize these moments to restore her energy. Everyone knows they need breaks throughout the day. How often do you schedule them on your calendar, just to ignore the notification and power right on through? Rather than telling Jasmine something she already knew, I needed to better understand why she didn't prioritize refueling her energy tank. The answer was twofold.

Our current culture generally glorifies being "busy" as if it's a badge of honor. People associate busy with working hard, and hard work with success. To shift Jasmine's perspective in redefining what success meant to her, I asked her to assess how effective she had been at attaining her goals in all aspects of her life by referencing a Wheel of Life.[2] In completing this exercise, Jasmine focused her attention on actions she could take to accomplish *her* goals of success versus external influences outside of her control.

Jasmine explained that she saw these breaks as luxuries and many times felt guilty when she took time for herself. She never defined these breaks as needs or non-negotiables. How often do you skip something you believe to be a nice-to-have versus a need? We do it all the time! For Jasmine to redefine these breaks as energetic needs versus amenities, or moments of self-care, she needed to quantify the impact of these rest stops. Over a course of two weeks, she solicited anonymous feedback from everyone around her about her presence, influence, communication, energy levels, and quality of work, never sharing which days she did and did not recharge. Numbers don't lie. Jasmine couldn't believe the scores reflected the same person. She was less impactful in her personal and professional life when she didn't prioritize her energetic needs. As someone who leads with level four energy and wants to be of service, she immediately saw that her decision to skip breaks was working against her rather than for her.

Now that Jasmine had fully bought into the importance of refueling, I asked her to detail everything that brought her joy and pleasure. She listed activities such as going for a walk. She loved FaceTiming with her goofy nieces and nephews. Motivational poems gave her energy to reflect and refocus. And a quick laugh with her partner always brought her joy. These little jolts of joy gave her something to look forward to, but even more importantly they refueled her energy tank so she could continue to offer the care and service she prided herself on providing.

By simply extending her meetings to reflect the actual time she desired to connect with others, organizing her calendar to energize her versus deplete her, and adding breaks that brought her joy and pleasure, Jasmine shifted from feeling exhausted to feeling balanced. This extra energy enhanced her concentration and increased her self-confidence and drive towards accomplishing her goals. She no longer made consistent errors and loved the enhanced quality of her work, something that was not even on her radar.

To ensure that Jasmine's personal life harmonized with her work life, we looked at two specific areas she identified as a challenge. Jasmine's past roles always took place in an office. Therefore, when she was done with work, she could take the time during her walk home to decompress from work mode before switching to personal and partnership mode. There was a concrete divide that Jasmine needed to recreate.

Jasmine's current role was remote, making it much more challenging to divide. She tried blocking off her calendar so others wouldn't schedule anything after 5:00 p.m. Unfortunately, Jasmine still had access to schedule meetings and was her own worst enemy with upholding this boundary. She tried closing her computer, shutting her office door, and turning off her phone, only to reopen any and all of these a few moments later. Does this sound like someone you know? Is that someone you?

Ultimately, the change of physical location at the end of the day created the energetic shift Jasmine needed. She shared her challenge with her workout community and built an infrastructure of accountability around her. By 5:30 p.m., she had to be out of the apartment to make it to her 6:00 p.m. scheduled class. Missing class would result in financial penalties; thus Jasmine never missed a class. Each night she returned home with excitement, as her class and workout gave her the energetic shift she needed to transition from being a leader to focusing on herself and her partner.

With her work and her partnership flowing smoothly, Jasmine was ready to tackle her last challenge. She hated saying no to anyone! It literally pained her, which is why she always said yes, even when she knew she couldn't be physically or mentally present in two places at once. My favorite and failproof recommendation for people who can't say no is to say yes!

Say yes to everything that brings you joy and aligns with your values and goals. Wondering what this looks and sounds like? Here are a few examples of questions that came Jasmine's way, and how she answered each to ensure her decisions and actions were in alignment with her goals:

Question 1: Jasmine, we would love for you to join our daughter's two-year-old birthday party this weekend! Carsyn is just so excited for her Barbie-themed extravaganza. There will be people from all over, and while we will be hosting and running around, it would be great to see you!

Jasmine's Response: Lydia, thank you so much for the invite! I am so excited for Carsyn to turn two years old. I would love to catch up with you another night to really spend time connecting on your life, hearing how Carsyn is doing, and sharing updates about my life. How about we look for a more intimate evening that works for us both!

Question 2: Jasmine, I am fed up with your father. He's only a month out of retirement and he's driving me crazy. Want to come home for the weekend to give me some personal space, and occupy your father?

Jasmine's Response: Mom, I love you, and I feel your frustration and desire to have more personal space now that Dad's newly retired. It's understandable this shift in schedule is difficult to navigate! How did you share your feelings with Dad? How did he respond to your feedback? I would love to come up and be a rock for both of you in the upcoming weeks as you continue to communicate and work through this new change. Call me back with Dad to ensure we are all aligned and can select a weekend that works best for us all.

Question 3: Sister, I am in from Paris! I can't believe I haven't been back to the US since the start of Covid. I know my trip is last minute, but I would love to see you while I pop into the States for a week.

Jasmine's Response: Brother, I miss you so much! I haven't seen you in so long and miss your mug. Let me look into making a few changes in my schedule so we can have Sunday all to ourselves. Let's make sure to get some of our favorite activities in, even if it's just for the day. Let's divide and conquer. I'll look up availability at Albi, and you look up which of our favorite museums are open this weekend to visit.

Two out of three of these examples resulted in a no; however, Jasmine said yes to what mattered most to her. By energizing your values, you gain confidence to make decisions that boost your energy and propel you towards your goals. Not sure what your values are, and how those drive your goals? Take my Values-Driven Solution Assessment[3] to give you clarity on what matters to you most, and how to energize each motivator to make values-aligned decisions throughout your life.

In less than nine months, Jasmine was excelling at her role, expanding her impact, and was offered the VP of HR role at her company. In addition to her energy excelling at work, her personal life continued to flourish as well. She found harmony in her relationships with friends and family, and she and her partner moved in together in September of 2021 and are planning to buy a home in the upcoming year.

In summary, once Jasmine prioritized her *own* energetic needs, she *then* was able to spend more time focusing on harnessing her leadership skills. In the upcoming sections of the service zone, I will dive into how leaders can use level four energy to motivate and manage their teams. From there, I will show how this constructive energy can also be used to shift policies, practices, and procedures to enhance any organization's energetic profile to lead with care.

Lesson 2: Empathize and Release

In 2021, Caesars Entertainment hired me to be the chief energy officer. In addition to consulting, my role included speaking twice monthly on how to shift their emerging leaders' energies from surviving to thriving using energetic principles at their Emerging Leader Summits across a variety of their 55 US-based properties. Each Emerging Leader Summit hosted three to five properties, with a total of around 50 team members and leaders coming together from various locations. Before the in-person event, the selected emerging leaders met for various virtual workshops, including a kickoff event, where I introduced them to the impact of understanding their personal energy at work. By the time we met in person, the group had completed a personal energy assessment and was excited to hear how their perspectives impacted their own energy levels, as well as those around them.

In June 2021, I was speaking at Horseshoe Tunica Hotel and Casino, when Jamal, a hotel front desk manager, shared a challenge he and his department were currently facing. Jamal's energetic profile showed he strongly led with level four energy, which Jamal explained was no surprise, as he and his team prided themselves on creating personalized and everlasting memories for every guest. To create these singular encounters, Jamal extensively trained his team on how to empathize with each customer to better anticipate their needs. Empathy is a strong emotion felt when connecting with someone coming from the service zone. The gift of this energy allows individuals not only to observe and listen, but to understand and see what another person is experiencing from their point of view.

Through Jamal's leadership, the front desk team not only sought out how each person preferred to be greeted throughout their stay, but they learned about their travels, the reason for their visit, their upcoming plans, and their interests. His success was echoed throughout the summit, as other departments leaned on the knowledge Jamal's team gained about their guests to personalize each point of their stay, from housekeeping to food and beverage. As we discussed earlier, the advantage of these personalized interactions, when positive, is that energy is contagious. Each time hotel operations learned about a guest's anniversary, birthday, conference, or the like, their energy increased, making it easy for them to create unique experiences showcasing their excellence in service.

The challenge was, when a guest arrived with negative energy, Jamal and team continued to empathize, taking on their customer's energy the same way. When a guest shared their frustrations and anger (level two), this anger spread like Covid-19 throughout their department, and even further into the operations of the resort! If a guest shared a difficulty they were facing, and a front desk attendant personally couldn't assist with their challenge, their energy often shifted to sorrow and self-doubt (level one). When those who lead with service don't believe they can provide quality service, the energy they gain from their expertise becomes depleted, leaving them irritated, annoyed, and detached from their work.

This example Jamal shared created a perfect opportunity to educate the entire roomful of leaders how the energetic principle of attaching and releasing could benefit each of their departments. To start, we celebrated Jamal's team's accomplishments. They were seen as top performers, and their insights led to consistent high satisfaction survey scores resulting in a high return-customer rate. Consistent comments from surveys included words such as memorable, compassionate, understanding, excellence, teamwork, and care. They were accomplishing their goal of creating extraordinary moments for their guests.

The opportunity lay in detaching from others' destructive energy. For visualization purposes, I had each team member put on an article of clothing from a colleague next to them. I wanted the room to see energy from another perspective. They had no problem pointing out which article of clothes was not theirs, so why was it hard to see when they wearing someone else's energy?

To broaden the scope outside of work, I also asked where else the group noticed they were wearing external energy. Numerous leaders quickly identified examples of our society's attachment to information. Technology today allows us to be updated constantly by social media and the news, creating an opportunity for our energy to be influenced by factors outside of our control. How many times have you let a social media post or news story affect your emotions and actions?

I personally shared that I never knew Kobe Bryant, and I rarely watch professional basketball. However, when I received the news that he and his daughter had passed, I went into mourning and took off work. The energy I carried from this empathy became crippling. If you don't gain the power to empathize and release, and consistently carrying everyone else's challenges as your own, your energy plummets, creating a bigger divide between you, your goals, and your positive impact.

By walking through actual examples that occurred at the front desk, each individual worked on identifying where they attached and empathized, but also where they had an opportunity to release. The goal was to empower the team to discover where they could take charge of their energy so they could control their thoughts, emotions, and ultimately their reactions. To start, every time a guest departed the front desk, each member asked themselves a series of questions:

1. Did I fulfill my role and provide excellent service to the best of my ability?

2. Is there any action item I have control over to enhance this guest's experience?

3. How did I feel before this guest interaction and after?

4. If the guest shared negative energy during our interaction, how do their life perceptions and experiences impact my life, choices, and journey?

5. How do I want to feel after this guest interaction?

By going through these five questions, the front desk team was able to see they were in charge of their emotions and reactions. In reviewing this example, how can you personalize these questions to your own day-to-day experiences to ensure you can attach and release? Explore how you connect with others and external factors, and where you can implement a process of reflection and ensure you choose your reaction. Over time, these questions become habitual, allowing you the space to continue to lead with service, enhancing your energy, engagement, and passion for providing quality work.

Lesson 3: Detach from Your Solution

Throughout our journey through the service zone, you've discovered that level four energy comes from a place of care. When choosing to lead with level four energy, and to ensure you can provide the best support to the greatest number of people, we walked through examples stressing the importance of prioritizing your energetic needs. An empty gas tank won't help anyone. A fully fueled car can take passengers exactly where they need to go.

You also recognized the power of leading with empathy and detaching from others' energy, the same way you can remove a borrowed article of clothing you no longer want to wear. In this final illustration, I will demonstrate how the energetic principle of detaching from your own solution can be used on an individual basis, a leadership basis, and even a companywide initiative to enhance your relationship with yourself, others, and your organization.

In October of 2016, I was hired to be the director of HR operations for Pinnacle Entertainment (PNK). PNK had acquired the Meadows Racetrack and Casino the month before and was still in integration mode from their previous acquisition of eight Ameristar properties from August of 2013. My role had been created due to a need to streamline HR policies and procedures. Each acquisition came with its own set of customs, and as PNK continued to grow they quickly saw the dichotomy across their 16 gaming and entertainment locations. Conflicting practices across the organization created inefficiencies, communication errors, and legal risk.

Before even receiving and accepting the offer, I interviewed with various leaders across HR, finance, F&B (food and beverage), hotel operations, and marketing. My interviews culminated with a final interview with PNK's CEO, Anthony Sanfilippo. Anthony is well known and highly respected in the casino industry. He served in various executive roles at Harrah's Entertainment, Inc., the world's largest casino company at the time. He was also known for pioneering innovative green initiatives at Harrah's, sustainable solutions that are now practiced across hotels worldwide. While I was of course impressed by the leaders I met across the business, PNK's national portfolio, strong financial statements, and Anthony's accomplishments, my biggest question was whether PNK was "walking the talk" when it came to their values.

Why was this question so important to me? My role was created to ensure PNK's portfolio shifted from operating as single units to one cohesive enterprise. How does a company ensure their communication, vision, and mission all align? By creating a cohesive strategy stemming from their values.

I learned this important lesson when I joined the Cosmopolitan of Las Vegas, Autograph Collection, Marriott (TCOLV), in 2010. At the time, I did not understand the importance of a values-driven culture because I had never had an experience with an organization that led by example. I had worked for and seen how organizations shared their company principles. But putting them into practice, within each and every department, procedure, communication, and policy, was quite another matter. TCOLV was exemplary in executing on their promise, coming directly from the top, with our CEO, John Unwin. After my time at TCOLV, I knew the power of a values-driven culture and how leading with values directly tied to the energy of an operation. This alignment became the most important factor in my decision to join, as it was my number one energetic need to ensure I could drive PNK forward to accomplish our unified goal of creating a united people operations strategy.

PNK's values were integrity, care, excellence, innovation, and ownership. To evaluate if PNK's operations and energy aligned with their values, throughout my interviews with various leaders, I asked how they placed each into practice. Naturally, different departments gravitated towards different values. Hotel operations leaned into excellence. Finance demonstrated their commitment to ownership. I could literally taste innovation when sampling the creations from F&B. And integrity was illustrated through each policy and procedure I reviewed. When I met with Anthony Sanfilippo, he highlighted how and why the organization chose each value, all stemming from his driving purpose. Anthony led with care.

I accepted the opportunity to join and jumped into my new role with vigor and excitement. Knowing PNK's mission and vision originated from level four energy, my priority as the director of HR operations was to ensure each HR function, tool, and resource across the entire enterprise came from a place of attention and concern for those impacted. Who did these practices impact? My customers, who were our team members, all 16,000 or so of them. How could I ensure every team member had a voice in the creation of our newfangled people processes? I prioritized our communication tools and concentrated on performance feedback specifically to ensure both leaders and their team members could weigh in on what they found most valuable in executing their job. How was performance feedback currently structured and solicited at this time? As I shared earlier, various properties had various methods. These ranged from SuccessFactors electronic accolades, performance evaluation automated and paper questionnaires, to on-the-job commentary sheets, including personal improvement plans (PIP) and disciplinary action forms.

After reviewing the variety of channels, my first step in ensuring that all feedback came from a place of care was to create one process and tool that empowered each team member's voice. The challenge was that, although some of the instruments used did foster two-way communication, the majority of the forms and methodology used were unilateral. After traveling from property to property and working with IT, HR, and operations leaders on creating a centralized process, I discovered that developing a unified resource was going to be the easiest step in my course of action. Changing leadership's mindset on consistently soliciting interpersonal communication to engage and energize their employees would take much more work.

To develop a companywide communication plan about the upcoming changes, I recognized that I needed to better understand how and why the current mindset around one-way feedback existed. Why was this understanding of past practices so important? Because I needed to certify how these changes would impact the organization from each leader's perspective. Honoring past perspectives would ensure I could communicate the "why" for the upcoming changes to ensure that all of PNK aligned on adopting one new perspective moving forward.

Here is what I learned. Leaders exhibit attributes of expertise and influence. Therefore, it's natural to assume a leader's experience would provide the best insights to address challenges quickly and effectively. In a fast-paced environment, such as these hotels and casinos, operating 24 hours, where challenges can arise at any given time, unilateral communication was created as an efficient was to provide immediate solutions to any team member in need. The one-way feedback systems and resources in place stemmed from care! And for years these worked and served their purpose. Questions resulted in answers. Problems resulted in resolutions. Follow the recipe, and results should follow.

If this formula worked in the past, then why were engagement scores declining? Why were Hotline complaints and investigations on the rise? Why was turnover increasing in various departments? Why was the energy around communication and feedback heavy? Here's why. In addition to generational differences with communication styles, a glaring drawback of leading with level four energy surfaced. Many times, those who love to be of service also love to solve problems. And while their expertise warrants them providing a solution, two potential challenges can arise:

Potential Challenge 1: Many times, what works for one person does not work for another. People come from diverse backgrounds, all influencing how they experience a situation. Additionally, people learn in different ways. If a leader provides an auditory direction and their team member learns kinesthetically, a lot can get lost in translation and execution. How do you think this impacts a leader's energy? They just provided a solution that didn't work for their team member! That can leave them feeling frustrated (level two) or inadequate (level one). How do you think this impacts a team member? They were given a solution that didn't work for them, which can leave them feeling annoyed (level two) or stupid (level one).

Potential Challenge 2: Have you had a child, or watched over a little one in your lifetime? If you have, I'm guessing that at one point you've gotten sucked into their throw-the-toy game. They throw. You fetch. They throw again. You fetch again. They throw a third time and laugh. You fetch a third time and growl. Quite quickly, the game stops being fun for the one who keeps on fetching. If you are a leader and provide an answer every time a team member asks a question, how much room do you think you are providing them to learn? Executing on exact directions is much easier than solving for a remedy. Additionally, if a person knows they can keep coming back for an answer, there's no consequence for not committing the answer to memory. While the initial response of providing an answer will be easier for a leader, allowing your team member to solution-orient over the long term will result in sustainable learning. (More tips and tricks on how to combat this challenge are coming up in Chapter 8, "The Curiosity Zone.")

After I shared these findings and insights with leaders, an energy shift occurred. This shift resulted in the creation of a coaching form, where team members and leaders shared their perspectives on their performance, with sections to celebrate their successes as well as to highlight opportunities. Discipline was removed from our vocabulary, companywide. Termination was no longer a selection box on our forms. If a separation occurred between a team member and employer, each understood why the separation happened, as multiple conversations would have already occurred on both sides. Coaching with CARE became our standard philosophy, empowering every voice across all of PNK.

Action Steps and Takeaways

1. Prioritize Yourself!
   - Do you notice yourself having energy in the morning, but crashing by the end of the day?
   - Are you constantly rushing from one thing to the next?
   - Do you place everyone else's concerns ahead of your own?
   - Are you the go-to person with whom people share their challenges?
   - Do you wish you had time for things that bring you joy and energy, but there just aren't enough hours in the day?

     How can you be of service if you have no more energy to give? If you answered yes to any of the above questions, explore where you can prioritize your energetic needs. By placing yourself energy first, you will gain more energy to give more energy, making you more impactful with purpose and passion!

2. Empathize and Release
   - Are you able to empathize with others, placing yourself in their perspective?
   - Do you notice yourself getting upset or sad after watching or reading the news?
   - How do you feel after you scroll through social media? Are you noticing any energy shifts causing judgment towards others or yourself?

   Empathy is a powerful gift that allows you to see others from their perspective. Embrace this gift to connect with others. Once the moment has passed, it's important to remember to release. Carrying others' frustration or sorrow can be debilitating, pulling you away from your goals and accomplishments.

3. Detach from Your Solution
   - Do you love to help others create solutions for their challenges?
   - Are your recommendations based on resolutions that worked for you?
   - Are you tired of the same people coming to you constantly with questions, and many times, with the same type of question?
   - Do you get upset if someone doesn't take your recommendation?

Final Thoughts

You have a talent for helping others, and make people feel welcomed and free of judgment to share their challenges. Listen, observe, and share your thoughts and insights. Remember, what works for you might not work for them. If you notice yourself getting frustrated or down because of another person's difficulty, take a moment to explore how you're imparting your perspectives on their situation. Explore where you can be supportive and allow them the space to find the answer that works best for them.

CHAPTER

8

The Curiosity Zone

I joined the Cosmopolitan of Las Vegas as a recruiter shortly after it opened in 2010. I aligned with the brand's vision of being "new and different that matters," and was excited to shake up the traditional employment culture at one of the strip's hottest new hotels and casinos.

Our recruitment ads and values mirrored our customer brand, targeting the "curious class" as a customer and employee, whom we called CoStars. Instead of wearing nametags and providing scripts, we promoted meaningful connections. Instead of finding fault for mistakes, we welcomed ingenuity and learned from each opportunity. Our ingenious approach created a diverse culture of community, transforming each candidate into a CoStar the moment a person joined our team.

Inclusive environments that cultivate curiosity foster creative solutions. Therefore, we designed an open forum, led by our CEO, John Unwin. On a monthly basis, we invited CoStars, no matter their title or position, to share recommendations to cross-collaborate on departmentwide challenges. When customer service noticed an uptick in concerns about the cleanliness of the casino floor, this open forum became the perfect event to test our organization's imagination.

How could we ensure the busy casino floor stayed clean? The traditional response would have been to hire more environment service workers (EVS). We had just opened our property, and we were operating in the red. There was no appetite to spend more money and increase headcount. Therefore, we led with curiosity and asked a few more questions to get us to our mark. How could we accomplish our goal without increasing headcount? How could we motivate everyone to chip in? Finally, what tools did we have in place to share this message?

The additional questions led to an energetic brainstorming session around our Intranet and artistic culture. The outcome resulted in a strategic campaign highlighting each CoStar's ingenuity. The campaign went viral! So much so that CoStars started to compete, looking for trash to one-up the next. A banquet member posted a video of himself cleaning a "dangerous" spill, featuring the song "Dangerous" by Kardinal Offishall. An intern posted a photo of himself and a Jell-O container with the tagline "Jell No you didn't take this out of Co!" (Co refers to our CoStar Dining Room.)

Before we knew it, the hotel was spotless! The energy of our inclusive environment plus the diversity of thought and free range to flow produced an inventive solution that was not only fun but also saved the company manpower and money. This is what I call a win-win. This is the power of the curiosity zone!

Service Zone Qualities: Curiosity, Growth, Understanding

Level five energy is a powerful constructive energy and is the first energy level where people lead with inquiry versus judgment. When leading with level five energy, you are able to view any situation as an opportunity to develop and expand your knowledge. This embodies the definition of curiosity, seeking to learn and grow.

How does one exhibit curiosity? Curiosity starts with demonstrating a growth mindset. The concepts of growth and fixed mindsets were originally developed by psychologist Carol Dweck to describe two different approaches people have toward their capabilities and capacity to learn. A person with a growth mindset believes that abilities and talents can be developed through commitment and staunchness. They view challenges as an opportunity to learn and continuously improve and believe that their brainpower and potential are not fixed.

Contrary to the growth mindset, those with a fixed mindset believe they are born with certain talents and skills. While they may believe you can continuously grow, they fix their growth to areas they are naturally good at. Due to their belief that they're "gifted" in only certain areas, they tend to evade areas where they aren't "gifted."

It's important to note that even though a person with a fixed mindset doesn't believe they can be developed outside of their comfort areas, with practice and energy, their perspective can shift. This learning is critical because our workforce is rapidly changing with a new generation that no longer tolerates a fixed mindset approach to DEIA, sustainability, work-life balance, and authenticity. Let's explore how individuals, groups, and organizations can cultivate curiosity through a growth mindset to enhance themselves, their teams, and the company.

Individuals

Lead with Curiosity to Fall Back in Love with Your Job

Over the last few years, you've likely either left a job or had someone leave your team. The Big Quit kicked off the Great Reshuffle, with record resignations nationwide. If you're a regular on LinkedIn, the posting "I'm happy to share that I've started a new position as TITLE at COMPANY" has flooded your feed. Each time someone posts about their new position and/or company, LinkedIn notifies your network and those within six degrees (Bacon's Law). To ensure you too can celebrate with your connection, a plethora of personalized congratulations are auto-populated for you to share your celebratory sentiments within seconds.

How much do you love celebrating your connection's announcements? Please, be authentic. My guess is that a few emotions come to mind when you see these posts:

A. Delight—genuine excitement!

B. Indifference—keep scrolling.

C. Curiosity—where did they go and why?

D. Ridicule—so the grass isn't always greener.

E. Fear—should I be making a move?

If you selected D or E, it's important to assess why you feel the way you do. If you have been in the same role, with the same company, or in the same industry for a bit of time, surges of lethargy are completely understandable. Are you feeling a bit bored at work? Are you missing the growth and challenge you felt when you first started your role?

If you recently started a new role and aren't feeling the excitement you expected, have you evaluated if it's in line with your values? What attracted you to the role in the first place? Whatever your situation, your connection with your work is similar to your personal relationships. Both require energy to keep the relationship exciting and stimulating.

So if any of these thoughts are permeating your mind, it's important to evaluate if it's time to move to a new job, industry, or career. If it's not, then the next question becomes, how can you fall in or back in love with your job? Before jumping into change, it's always important to assess your current energy level and vantage point. How can you fall back in love with your job and your work? Lead with curiosity to invigorate what excites you most. Here are four questions to initiate your discovery of falling back in love:

Question 1: What interested you about your role or industry in the first place?

Many times, we get caught in our routines and forget what initially attracted us to our job. Make a list of the items that originally interested you about your role. Highlight areas you are no longer experiencing. If these areas bring you joy and excitement, create an action plan to integrate them back into your work.

Question 2: What items can you offload to ensure you can add growth opportunities to your workload?

If you don't feel like you have the capacity to add more to your workload, it's time to do an audit. What needs to be offloaded? What have you outgrown that you are still doing out of routine? As you grow, so do your responsibilities. Identify and delegate items that will encourage others on your team, so you can continue to develop in new areas too.

Are you operating efficiently? Or are doing something the same way it's always been done? Ensure that your processes are streamlined so you aren't exerting wasted energy on a process that can be easily tightened up, digitalized, or automated.

Question 3: Where can you become an expert in your field?

Once you understand your responsibilities and how to effectively execute your projects, it's easy to become complacent. Becoming an expert takes work, dedication, and concentration. What more can you learn about your role? Are there courses that can provide you with greater knowledge? Is there a conference within the next year that can energize you to provide you with insights into how you can dive deeper? Take this opportunity to celebrate your accomplishments, then ask yourself what else you can learn to continue to grow.

Question 4: How does your role give you purpose?

In every job you take, it's important to ensure you understand how your responsibilities tie to your overall mission or purpose. This exercise might appear to be easy for some roles compared to others. For example, let's look at a teacher's purpose. Their purpose could be to increase emotional well-being for future generations. What if your job is to deliver packages? Amazon does a great job of sharing their employees' purpose, from the moment a package is ordered until it's delivered. No matter what role you're in, ensure you see how your actions impact your final consumer and highlight each impact you create that energizes your passion and purpose.

As the LinkedIn notifications continue to permeate your news feed, think about these questions to ensure your reaction triggers joy versus aggravation. Anyone can run from job to job. It takes focused energy to reflect, explore, and perfect your craft. Cultivate curiosity to make calculated moves that energize you to success with authentic and commemorative celebrations!

Lead with Curiosity to Get the Raise or Promotion You Want

Every year, companies around the world initiate engagement surveys and performance reviews, highlighting the successes of the year, as well as opportunities for the following year. While each evaluation primarily highlights and evaluates the past months or the full year, it's most important for leaders and individuals to have authentic conversations about their future goals and desires.

Are you excited to connect with your leader about a promotion opportunity? Are you hoping to ask for a raise, but not sure how to approach the conversation? Lead with curiosity and follow these three steps to ensure you effectively communicate your worth and requests.

Step 1: Evaluate Your Worth

Do you know your market data? Do the research you need to collect this data to have a true understanding of your desired role and its market worth. Not sure where to access the most accurate information? Start with compensation tools such as payscale.com, mercer.com, salary.com, and glassdoor.com to see what information has been published. Interested in having a conversation with someone to validate the data you collected? Conduct a few informational interviews. Reach out to people in your industry or people who have the role you desire. This conversational narrative will complement the data you will acquire from the tools mentioned above.

Is your organization strapped for cash at present? Explore additional areas you can add to your compensation outside of a traditional base salary. Does your role tie to revenue or business development? If so, can you increase your commission structure based on the business you bring in? Are there any networking tools that could assist you with building more business? If so, ask if your organization can pay for your costs to join associations, business networking groups, or country clubs. Most companies have money allocated for learning and development. What courses are you interested in that can add to your continuous growth? Are there any certifications you could obtain to propel you forward? Have you used all your wellness dollars?

If not, see what qualifies under wellness. Most wellness programs include gym memberships and coaching support as part of their programs. The opportunities outside of traditional compensation are endless—so much so that I did a TEDx[1] talk on this exact topic, encouraging employees and organizations to elevate and innovate their benefits and compensation offerings to create a total rewards suite, creating a motivational workplace culture based on transparency and personalization.

Step 2: Know Your Values

Why is taking a values assessment so important? When you know your values and have taken the time to uncover what matters to you the most and define it in your own words, you will have a surge of energy and confidence to communicate what matters to you most.

How can you incorporate your values into your ask? Here are a few examples to help you brainstorm what this will sound like for you:

- "One of my values is excellence and based on my consistent performance of excellence, my worth is $100,000 annually."

- "I value time with my family and would like to discuss hybrid options as part of my new schedule for 2024."

- "I would like to explore long-term investment opportunities available through the organization to ensure I honor my value of security for myself and my family."

Step 3: Communicate Your Value Proposition

While your direct leader knows your impact on the organization, many times they also must explain this impact to finance, compensation, or your new department of interest. Use the following three questions to organize your accomplishments so your manager can easily and effectively showcase your value proposition.

Question 1: What have you accomplished?

Question 2: What tools or resources did you use to execute your success?

Question 3: How did this impact the organization?

Here is an example to showcase what this looks and sounds like:

What I accomplished: I updated our manual paper transfer process to an automated digital workflow process.

What tools and resources I used to execute this success: I collaborated with HR systems to activate and personalize the workflow process tool available within our HRIS, which wasn't previously being used.

How this impacted the organization: This process change reduced our transfer time from an average of four weeks to two days and saved the organization an average of $6,923.16/role.

Put it all together: I updated our manual paper transfer process to an automated digital workflow process by collaborating with HR Systems to activate and personalize the workflow process tool available within our HRIS, that wasn't presently being used. This process change reduced our transfer time from an average of four weeks to two days and saved the organization an average of $6,923.16/role.

Leaders

How Curiosity Can Instill Confidence in Your Employees

Growing into a leadership role is a great accomplishment. Leaders attain higher responsibilities for their department's initiatives and become the motivational energy for their organization. When you're a leader, providing solutions to challenges based on your experience and expertise is a gift you can provide your team. While this gift can bring you joy and passion for your role, do you ever find yourself exhausted by the end of the day just from helping everyone else? Here are three recommendations on how to lead with curiosity to instill confidence in your employees, resulting in more time and energy back to you!

Recommendation 1: Focus on the Solution Versus How Your Team Arrives There

Your role and responsibility as a leader are directly tied to your department and organization's success. This direct correlation naturally invests you in making the right choices. The challenge is that, while your solution works for you, this doesn't mean it will work for everyone.

The first step in leading with curiosity to build confidence in your team starts with detaching yourself from how your team arrives at the end solution. Allow your team to design their own route to success. If you see their route isn't the most efficient or effective, ask them what opportunities they learned throughout their experience.

If they ask you for recommendations that worked for you, share those! Sharing your experience does not mean that they must or even will follow your path. It just means that they are continuing to explore a diverse set of paths to determine what best suits them. By allowing your team to choose what works best for them, your energy can be repurposed to focus on leading versus managing.

Recommendation 2: Respond with Questions Versus Answers

It is completely natural to provide an answer to a question. As a leader, you have already experienced many of the same challenges your team is facing. Providing an answer on the spot is the easiest and fastest way to mitigate an urgent problem.

While a solution might resolve an immediate need, when you solve a person's problem, you take away an opportunity for them to learn and grow. How can you lead with questions to help your team find answers that solve their problems? Observe how I change answers to questions in the following scenario:

Employee: Leader, I am so excited about our new acquisitions. My challenge is that all of my energy is going to each merger and acquisition (M&A) and I noticed I haven't been able to keep up with my daily tasks that are required of my primary role.

Leader (Response with Answers): Thank you for bringing your concerns to my attention. I completely understand how new acquisitions can be sucking up your time and energy.

1. Identify the tasks you haven't been able to complete.

2. Evaluate who else knows how to do those items and delegate accordingly.

3. If you can't identify anyone to take on these responsibilities, reach out to team members who expressed interest in growth assignments and train them on how to accomplish these undertakings, and provide them with oversight.

Leader (Response with Questions):

1. What tasks are you following behind on in your role?

2. How else can we ensure those items get completed if you aren't able to complete them?

3. Is anyone else on the team able to assist? If not, has anyone else on the team, or other teams, expressed interest in learning these duties?

4. Would you be interested in training others on how to complete these duties?

5. What other innovative ideas do you have to rectify this situation?

Please give yourself grace; this exercise takes time. Each time you catch yourself reacting to an answer, take a deep breath and take a moment to question your natural reaction. Ask: how can I change this answer into a question? Your questions will help your team look at their challenges from a different viewpoint, giving them an opportunity to find the solution that best suits them.

Recommendation 3: Inspire Your Team to Present Solutions with Their Challenges

As employees practice finding their own solutions through your leadership questions, they will start to gain confidence in providing direct resolutions. There are multiple advantages to this approach:

- The first advantage of this exercise is that their working decisions will continue to free you up from managing to leading and strategizing.

- As your team continues to grow, so do you, creating a strong succession pipeline.

- By allowing them the space to explore, you build psychological safety, so they continue to redefine success through growth opportunities.

- As you inspire your team to present as many viable solutions as possible to their challenges, you're motivating them to be creative and innovative.

- By motivating them to present solutions, they learn the business.

All of these advantages lead to increased engagement towards accomplishing an individual's, team's, and company's vision, mission, and goals.

Cultivate Curiosity to Align Opposing Employees on Your Team

A company's success is never accomplished by just one person. Success of that magnitude takes collaboration, because energy is exchanged collaboration, creating a catapult effect for individuals, allowing them to flow through ideas, solutions, and project plans.

For solo entrepreneurs, a collaboration of ideas might have occurred to envision your business. For larger organizations, your foundation might have started on a napkin among friends or colleagues, foreseeing a concept of something different, better, and innovative.

Of all the stories leading up to conception, one rarely hears of a group of people creating something magnificent when combative. Therefore, it's natural to ask, "What happens when you are asked to collaborate with someone with whom you don't get along?" When a group of people is resonating at a high level of energy, working towards the same vision and mission, creation occurs. How do you foster collaboration and creativity when your team is coming from opposing sides?

Here are three recommendations you can take to ensure you achieve success, even if you have opposing employees on your team.

Recommendation 1: Lead with Curiosity to See Where Your Team's Similarities Lie, Even If They're on "Opposing Sides"

When you see your team is divided, or two people believe they are completely different from each other, it's natural for them to hyperfocus and point out all their differences. What if they used that energy to focus on their similarities? As their leader, you're able to take a 360-degree view of opposing sides and see where these similarities lie. Use that information to foster moments of alignment rather than opposition. By focusing on each other's similarities, their energy can align to focus on your shared vision and mission.

Recommendation 2: Cultivate Curiosity to Ensure Your Team Respects One Another's Values

One of the most effective exercises an incohesive team can do is a values assessment. Once each person identifies and defines their values, the group can share what matters most to each person. Consistently, teams will see that many share the same values, or have the same definition for different values. When adversaries have different definitions or values, and these values are communicated, each side can collaborate by respecting and honoring each person's values while working alongside each other towards the same goal.

Recommendation 3: Get Curious on How Diversity of Thought Can Be Used as an Advantage rather than Disadvantage

Diversity of thoughts is one of the most powerful tools any team can leverage. As their leader, create space for your employees to explore their inherent biases and prejudices. By doing so, you can foster an environment of psychological safety for people to question each other and grow. The more opinions are respected from alternate perspectives, the more inclusive your environment. Bonding over differences can be just as powerful, if not more powerful, than bonding over similarities.

Leverage your team's opposing viewpoints to focus on challenges occurring within your products, services, processes, and customer service. When people from diverse backgrounds and perspectives collaborate, they are more likely to generate creative approaches that can lead to innovative problem-solving solutions. By creating a common bond in fixing a problem, you can activate diverse learning perspectives to improve your products, services, processes, and communication.

Organizations

Lead with Curiosity to Build a Motivational Workplace Culture

How inclusive is your organization? How psychologically safe do your employees feel to voice their ideas, questions, and concerns? How often do you solicit feedback from your employees? How often does their feedback drive change? For companies to build a motivational workplace culture, they must humanize the workforce, and engage in two-way communication. How can this be accomplished?

People Services

I have been fortunate to work for companies that understand that their number one asset is their people. So much so that the Cosmopolitan of Las Vegas and Allegiant Airlines didn't even call our department human resources (HR) but rather the "People and People Services Department." Whatever you choose to call the traditional HR function, it's imperative that this function be set up for success to lead the people strategy.

This means that HR not only has a seat at the table but is a business partner to the organizations, aligning your human capital strategy to the business strategy. Carrie Matthews, director of People Operations at 10Pearls, explains why this is so important. "When HR is involved from the onset, they are able to ensure what the organization is committing to is executable from a people perspective and aligns with the company values. If an organization establishes a strategy that doesn't take into account the day-to-day employee experience, the strategy will fail."[2]

By aligning your business strategy to your people strategy, your business will have a competitive advantage, directly linked to an increase in engagement, productivity, and revenue. How can your people function and execute on these deliverables? Personalize your organization's policies, procedures, and practices so that each are developed and supported not only from the top down, but also from the bottom up, aligning an organization across all levels.

Personalization

One size fits all didn't work in retail, and it's quite clear it doesn't work in the workplace. Personalization is becoming more and more prevalent in the workplace, and still has opportunity to grow. Individuals respond best when their wants and needs are specifically addressed. How has your company humanized your workplace?

This starts right from the beginning, with the interview evaluation process. Your candidates are interviewing you as much as you are interviewing them. Are you listening to their questions? Are you asking them about their wants and needs to ensure your business evolves with the people running the operation? This emphasis on personalization must continue into their respective departments throughout their onboarding. Do you conduct employee surveys? Open feedback sessions? How do you take employee feedback and create action plans to ensure your company walks the talk, and isn't just wasting their time to check a box?

Develop options for every program so employees can select what works best for them, ensuring everyone benefits from the opportunities you offer. From there, empower your employees to get involved with these action plans, so they can design policies, practices, and processes that work best for them to accomplish their goals, which in turn drives organizational success towards your company goals, vision, and mission.

Lead with Curiosity to Create Innovative and Sustainable Solutions to Address Your Staffing Needs

"In a boundaryless world, work isn't defined by jobs, the workplace isn't a specific place, and many workers aren't traditional employees."[3] How can organizations succeed in this ever-changing environment that no longer supports the structure and foundations they were built upon? Deloitte provides three answers. The first is "Think like a researcher." How does a researcher think? They lead with curiosity to seek to learn and grow.

As I consult with organizations around the world to address staffing shortages, I electrify them to lead with curiosity to develop innovative solutions that will build sustainable solutions to address their staffing needs. How can you think like a researcher to do the same? Here are some questions to explore as an organization:

1. When was the last time you reviewed your job descriptions? Are you posting a boring laundry list of to-dos that limit a person from applying versus welcoming someone to be curious to learn more about the opportunities you have and the culture you foster?
   - Update your postings to ensure skills, not just experience or degrees, are welcome.
   - Market yourself to candidates with passion, even if they don't meet all your desired credentials.
   - Get creative! Post videos of a job, share firsthand stories of those within those roles, and mention how they created the position to work for them.

- Ask your employees if they were a candidate, how they would want to learn about the specific tasks and duties. Don't filter; show the good, the great, the bad, and the ugly. In this information-sharing world, it will get out anyway. So get ahead of it, be authentic, and attract talent to the authentic you!

2. Show them your worth! How does your organization market its value and culture?
   - What should you include in this suite?
     - Traditional compensation: base salary/bonus/commissions/stock options.
     - Wellness dollars: compensation allocated towards physical and mental health; coaching, trainings, certifications, learning and development, gym memberships, country club memberships, doctor's visits, pet insurance, family leave, and so forth. These offerings are limitless!
     - Flexibility: What's your PTO policy? Your remote policy? Hybrid policy?

3. Lead with your values so you attract diverse talent that aligns with your values! And they will know you will foster a culture of inclusion and psychological safety, no matter their background.

4. Be proactive. Everyone loves to feel wanted, even if they don't reciprocate the same sentiment. Pipeline. Call. Text. Email. If a candidate had the confidence to apply, give them some credit. Too many have received auto rejection letters as soon as they apply. Address their fears and boost their confidence. You already know they have been successful before.

5. Speak to their motivators. Take the courageous step of asking people what they want in order to succeed. Most will respond with shock at first, because they've never been asked.

Once they get past the shock and realize you aren't joking, they will respect that you are honoring what works for them and will ensure they respect what you also need from them.

These tips will help your company attract and retain the talent that will not only give you that fresh start but will catapult you into the future.

Action Steps and Takeaways

In reviewing these examples, how can you cultivate curiosity to approach a challenge you're experiencing in your workplace?

Individuals: How and where can you take ownership of your workplace experience? If you ask yourself this question and respond with fingers pointed at everyone else, turn your finger around back at yourself. How can *you* control your narrative? Where can you take responsibility for what you're experiencing? How can you lead with curiosity to shift your energy from negative to positive?

Leaders: How effective a leader are you? If you can't answer that question, ask your team. If you're too exhausted to provide leadership to your team, lead with curiosity to ask: why? What shifts can you make to ensure you can provide strategy, guidance, growth, and support to enhance both your own and your team's energy?

Organizations: How energized is your workforce? If you don't know, it's time to conduct an internal and external assessment of your company. Is your organization operating in the constructive zone, or the destructive zone? Why are people staying? Why have people left? What policies and practices need to be adjusted to ensure you're fostering a motivated workplace culture?

Final Thoughts

Jump into exploring the power of curiosity! What shared tools can you use to immediately increase your own personal energy? How can you cultivate curiosity to shift the energy around you, whether on your team or within your organization? Use the chapter's key takeaways and action steps to motivate yourself, your team, and your organization with confidence and ease.

Please note, as with every zone, each level of energy comes with advantages and disadvantages. Now that we've entered the constructive zone, the disadvantages are limited; however, they are still important to highlight. How can level five energy be disadvantageous? When you see the world through a lens of opportunity, you're less fearful of making a mistake.

Mistakes become a part of the growth and learning journey! However, this doesn't mean you should jump into any opportunity that comes your way. Those who lead with level five energy take more risks. My caution, when leading with this energy, is to ensure you still have checks and balances in place, whether through a process or within your team. Taking a calculated risk is very different from jumping off a cliff and assuming you'll have a second opportunity to practice what you learned.

CHAPTER
9
The Creative Zone

In January 2009, I spent a month in Norway consulting for Radisson Blu Hotel & Resorts. I started down south in Kristiansand and worked my way up via Stavanger to Oslo. I continued north through Alesund and Trondheim, ultimately finishing my tour crossing the fjords via train, ending my time in Norway at my favorite northern lights fishing town, Tromso.

Every winter, pods of killer whales migrate to northern Norway, specifically around Tromso, in search of herring. As a cohesive team, they've created a hunting strategy called carousel feeding, enclosing the herring into a "bait ball," which occurs when fish are tightly packed into a spherical formation. From there, they work together to slap the fish with their tails so that they can pick them off one by one, ensuring the entire family is fed.

National Geographic photographer Brian Skerry swims with these magnificent creatures from Norway to New Zealand, Patagonia to South Africa. He shares incredible footage and insights on the cohesiveness of these apex predators and how their collaborative cultures are not so different from our own. So much so that they have diverse tastes, communication styles, and traditions based on their locations all over the world!

In an Earth Day episode podcast on April 13, 2021, Skerry explained the synergy of these mammals' operation. "It can be very vocal. . . . In fact, as that polar night emerges and it's dark all the time, they can no longer rely on just sight or visual cues, and they have to communicate. So, you hear these clicks and whistles and cacophony of sounds that are all around you."[1] Additionally, Skerry explained that he must be in tune with his energy because the killer whales are hypersensitive to a new energy entering their space, so when possible, he free dives versus using scuba gear to ensure he doesn't disrupt their operation.

Ultimately, Skerry highlights how similar killer whale culture is to ours. As I listened to Skerry's podcast, I thought back to my favorite times at work. I have so many moments that truly bring a smile to my face. But when I contemplate when I was most in synergy with my team and work, I think back to my time at Allegiant Airlines.

In 2014, I was poached from the Cosmopolitan of Las Vegas to bring my hospitality expertise to Allegiant Airlines, a low-cost carrier known for providing travel options to people from remote locations to vacation destinations. Allegiant's business model thrived on not competing—so much so that the company bragged about the fact that their only competition was their ideal customer's living room couch! Unfortunately, customer service scores suffered because of this sentiment. As Allegiant continued to scale and went public, they realized their current approach to customer service wasn't a sustainable model, as review after review echoed customer service concerns.

My first step upon starting my role was to evaluate the talent acquisition and employment services process from application to onboarding. As with any internal audit investigation, I unveiled hidden rocks of opportunities. These opportunities ranged from quick fixes to heavy lifts. Upon presenting my findings, I was approved to increase my team's size from seven to seventeen, showing how dedicated Allegiant was to shifting their customer's experience and narrative.

This team became my pod. We developed traditions, communication styles, and celebrations that echoed those of Skerry's orcas. Within one year of being a full team, and working in sync, we got recognized by Glassdoor. We were awarded Best Places to Interview, and I was featured as a guest speaker on "Hire Better Talent Faster: How to Optimize Your Employer Brand and Candidate Apply Process," where I shared the power of our energy, stemming from the creative zone.

Creative Zone Qualities: Creativity, Collaboration, Flow

The feeling of this energy zone, with level six energy, is synthesis. When you're experiencing the creative zone, you feel in sync and in flow with yourself and your surroundings, and your energy is highly constructive. When a person is experiencing level six energy, many feel tuned into their intuition and can tap into their creative talent. Level six energy becomes a gateway to innovation and is apparent within organizations that foster collaborative environments. This chapter explains how we developed, collaborated, and expanded our energy at Allegiant Airlines, shifting our brand's feedback from negative to positive.

Challenge 1: Customer Service

As I mentioned, in 2014 I was brought onboard Allegiant Airlines as their manager of Talent Acquisition and Employment Services.

The Cosmopolitan of Las Vegas taught me the power of bringing hospitality to the candidate and employee process. When your talent acquisition (TA) experience leads with hospitality, your employees naturally pass that energy along to your customers. Therefore, I recruited additional talent from industries that lead with the customer in mind, hiring recruiters and employment specialists with backgrounds from call centers, restaurants, retail, and entertainment. By developing a diverse team from various backgrounds and integrating them into a team of experts in the travel industry, we were able to share best practices from various perspectives to develop a one-of-a-kind talent acquisition experience for each of our talent verticals.

Our flight attendant recruitment process upgraded from the standard application to interview, to a multilayered experience. You see, when we opened our flight attendant requisitions, we had applications in the thousands coming in within days! Initially, there was no way we could review every application. Applicants applied, and if they met the minimum qualifications, they received a phone interview. If they passed the phone interview, they were asked to attend an in-person interview. Based on this process, take a guess at how many applicants could be reviewed weekly? Not many! And even if that recruiter did get through a chunk of volume a day, how much time could they really spend truly evaluating each person? The process was riddled with time constraints, volume constraints, fatigue, and unconscious bias.

To combat these challenges as a team, we collaborated and got creative. We added an assessment on the front end to ensure each applicant passed the minimum qualifications to be an Allegiant flight attendant before becoming a candidate. Questions included: Are you located at an Allegiant base that you could fly out of daily? This was unique to Allegiant versus the rest of the industry. Our business model offered flights to and from each base location. Major carriers not only fly across the nation, but most also fly internationally. Because of their multiple destinations and layovers, their talent can reside anywhere, so long as they can hop on a plane to work. Other questions included: Can you swim? Are you comfortable sliding out of a potentially crashing plane? Can you fit in a McDonnell Douglas MD-80 jump seat? There are height and width requirements for various planes, which was important to call out, because our planes were older and refurbished from overseas.

If a candidate passed these questions, they continued onto a video interview. By adding an assessment and video interviews to the front end of the application process, we were able to effectively handle the volume of interest, ensuring we could review every application we received. Flight attendants in the field caught wind of these changes and got so energized that they asked how they could help!

In response to their interest, we developed a Flight Attendant Recruitment Team to support our corporate recruiter. We trained the Flight Attendant Recruitment Team on TA practices, unconscious bias, compliance, and interview evaluation protocols. They reviewed the video interviews, deciding who got invited to in-person events nationwide. From there, the recruitment team joined in with the corporate TA team on group interviews and one-on-ones. Being a member of the Flight Attendant Recruitment Team became a coveted role. They were compensated for their additional hours at market rate for a flight attendant recruiter and took pride in the fact that they were building the next generation of flight attendants for Allegiant Airlines.

These flight attendants became so proud of their input, they also became part of the creative process. They designed specific swag to showcase their specialty. This swag sparked curiosity in our customers, exposing ideal employees we didn't even know existed within our customer base! Based on customer in-person feedback, we created an auto-survey in our applicant tracking system (ATS) to solicit feedback on the process from every one of our candidates, ensuring we fine-tuned and continuously improved every step of the TA experience.

In less than six months, we saw customer service scores increase, time to fill decrease, turnover decrease, and engagement increase. The success of this new TA process became a catalyst to look at all customer service roles, integrating changes to flight operations, call center, and ground operation recruitment workflows. But that's not even what energized and excited us the most. We expected measurable success in each of those areas upon shifting models and focus.

What we didn't expect was to get letters and emails from candidates we declined to move forward with, thanking us for a wonderful TA experience. Many shared that they would apply again in six months, the timeframe we required for candidates to wait to reapply. This unsolicited feedback became so abundant, we created an entire wall in our office displaying comments from candidates nationwide, celebrating our success.

Challenge 2: Pipeline Talent

In November of 2014, Allegiant Airlines announced they would be substantially expanding their outreach in the first quarter of 2015 with 18 new routes, including service to six new cities.[2] As we continued to grow, we knew how important it was to ensure we built sustainable pipelines to support our growing operations. Although we had pipelining needs in various areas of the operation, and pioneered solutions for each, I am going to share what I believed to be our most innovative process upgrade, as it directly aligned with Allegiant's core value of innovation.

Our pilots snickered at this message, but it was a running "joke" that Allegiant Airlines was an information technology (IT) company that happened to fly airplanes. Organizations worldwide struggle with finding pipeline talent for IT. Finding talent in Las Vegas was even more of a challenge. We directly competed with tech hubs out of Silicon Valley, surrounding up and coming tech cities such as Salt Lake City, Denver, and Austin, and mega resorts and casinos. Therefore, we had to get creative.

Lauren Burke Bennet was our IT talent advisor at the time and jumped at the opportunity to collaborate with innovative communities. She joined think tanks, partnered with organizations such as Dice, and hosted IT TA "speed dating" interview events on campus. As her leader, I encouraged her to push boundaries and pilot innovative solutions, even ones that the industry might not have thought about. Stemming from energetic brainstorming sessions, her curiosity sparked an inventive solution to pipelining IT talent.

In partnership with Iron Yard, a technology education company, Allegiant Airlines developed a pipeline education program to ensure students learned our curriculum in their classrooms. This partnership became fruitful for a variety of reasons:

1. Brand Awareness: Students gained access to learn about Allegiant Airlines core values and company culture working directly with our IT teams while in school. Like an internship, this gave both hiring managers and the students time to evaluate if they were a good fit.

2. Education: Students gained direct access to our curriculum, giving them an advantage over others applying for roles at our organization post-graduation. If hired, they could jump right into responsibilities, as they had already been trained on our way of doing things as a software engineer.

3. Cost Savings: To ensure students, schools, and Allegiant Airlines didn't pick up all training costs, we applied to state-funded and scholarship programs that supplemented costs for on-the-job training (OJT).

The success of these school partnerships allowed us to properly forecast our hiring needs to meet the demands of Allegiant Airline's growing business model. Once again, our success was celebrated companywide. Like flight attendant recruiting, the energy we created from this model became a catalyst to create programs within maintenance and flight operations magnet programs across the valley.

Challenge 3: Automation

For a pilot to be hired, they must pass several safety checks in addition to having the qualifications required for the role. These safety checks include a background check, a Department of Transportation (DOT) drug test, training evaluations, and the Pilot Records Improvement Act of 1996 (PRIA). The PRIA is industry-specific, and very different from traditional recruitment, as most jobs do not allow for employment records to be shared from company to company. In the airline industry, commercial air carriers must ensure they review at least five years of a pilot's background and safety records from previous employment.

At the time, this process was completely manual. Employment services would create a personnel file for each pilot candidate, collect their forms, and then would start emailing and calling, one by one, each previous employer to obtain their records. As you can imagine, this method was extremely tedious. Employment services had to observe time requirements, ensuring they followed up if they didn't hear back from a past employer. Each time they reached out, they had to log their attempt, contact info, date, and time, on the pilot's personnel file. Ultimately these files were used as audit trails for internal audit and the Federal Aviation Administration (FAA). As Allegiant continued to expand, it was clear this manual process was not sustainable and was a safety risk we were not willing to take.

Unfortunately, most processes throughout the business, all the way from the airport to the FAA, were manual. Therefore, it was no surprise that no one questioned the efficiency of the manual PRIA workflow. That is, until I asked why it needed to be done this way. At that moment, I realized I had the resources on my team to think through this problem differently. At the time, Cherika Best was the supervisor of Talent Acquisition and Employment Services. She had grown up in the airline industry and was a known expert in the field. In exposing Cherika to various software solutions from my time in hospitality, an energetic shift occurred. The team was finally granted the freedom to lead with curiosity and question each and every manual practice. Now remember, Allegiant Airlines is a low-cost carrier. So we knew there wouldn't be an appetite for expensive new software. Therefore, we took this opportunity to get creative to implement an innovative and efficient solution.

Cherika dove right in and sampled a variety of tools. In sharing the most suitable pieces of each instrument, we collaborated with IT to see how we could build our own automated tracking system to work smarter and not harder. Smartsheet became our answer! Smartsheet is a modern work management solution that allows cross-functional collaboration. How you use it, though, is up to the end users. Cherika jumped at the opportunity to streamline workflows. She took tutorials and training to learn the instrument's ins and outs and tailored them to our PRIA needs. The workflow we developed within employment services became so well recognized that, once again, the news and energy of our success spread companywide, and we were even recognized by the FAA for our ingenuity and received a 100% compliance rating from our PRIA Audit.

Constructive energy is contagious, and the news traveled fast. In less than six months, in partnership with human resources (HR) systems and information technology (IT), we automated all workflows. We went from personal action forms (PAFs) flying all over the country, waiting for a return signature, to signatures arriving at the click of a button from anywhere across the nation. This resulted in a substantial decrease in our time to fill metrics, directly increasing Allegiant Airline's bottom line.

In reflecting on this period, I smile at how much we grew as individuals, as teams, and as a company. I honestly thought HR systems and IT would have hated me for challenging them so much, but the opposite occurred. It became an exciting time. By challenging past practices, the team was able to realize how manual, inefficient, and unscalable our practices actually were, because they had been working so hard to make them work.

Each time a team hit a dead end, we challenged that dead end. From there, we all started to realize the seemingly undoable was actually very possible. In fact, we started to realize it was impossible not to automate our processes. Why would we choose to continue to work so hard for less than optimal results? That realization was so powerful.

It created a shift in how we approached and designed everything we did. Every challenge we conquered created this amazing energy, and it was contagious. What would have once been a daunting and overwhelming problem became challenging and exciting. Because of these automations, we received invitations to speak at conferences nationwide to share best practices at the request of Frontier Airlines, JSX, and United Airlines, to name a few.

Throughout the Allegiant Airlines success stories, consistent themes emerged, directly tied to level six energy. These themes included presence, collaboration, and flow, which all resulted in creative solutions to each of our challenges. Let's start with presence. What does it mean to be present? Being present comes from a state of mindfulness, which fuels your mental, physical, and emotional well-being. Being present allows you to be fully engaged with what you are experiencing, connecting you to yourself, as well as to those around you.

Presence is about showing up 100%. When you are present, you aren't distracted by external forces, such as your phone, outside noise, a squirrel . . . you are tuned in. I like to use the movie *Avatar* to symbolize this connection. When the characters connect their "Na'vi queues" to Pandora, this creates an energetic connection between them and their universe. The same goes for us humans. By showing up 100%, you become present and aware of your thoughts and emotions. The awareness of these thoughts and emotions becomes your drivers that lead you to action in alignment with your values, goals, purpose, and passion.

In writing this chapter, I naturally reached out to my former Allegiant Airlines team members to ensure I recapped each area thoroughly and succinctly. In conversations with Alex Cheney, he shared the following, "Driving the revamp of the flight attendant interview processes remains one of the biggest highlights of my career, and I am grateful I was given the opportunity to bring best practices to Allegiant Airlines. Not only did you, Rebecca, build a team of diverse backgrounds, but you empowered us to own our specific areas."[3] This ownership Cheney highlights is a key piece of practicing presence.

Each recruiter became immersed in their departments. The goal was for them to shadow their respective areas, and then get into the mindset of the role they recruited for. I wanted them to think like "their" team. Feel like "their" team members. Get curious about "their" pain points and excitement areas. By becoming present with their groups, they then could effectively recruit and solution orient for each of their departments. Cheney continued our conversation: "Our presence fostered an innovative environment where we got to learn from each other." These learnings from each other led to bonds of trust not only within recruitment, but in building a motivational workplace culture.

How so? Ashley McTaggart, flight operations recruiter, is a prime example. She tuned into flight operations her first week of joining Allegiant Airlines as a new flight operations recruiter. Her father-in-law was an Allegiant pilot, giving her insight into their department and industry's culture. If you've recruited for flight operations, you understand this group's attitude and energy. They are polished, confident, and disciplined. They hold hundreds of passengers' lives in their hands, while accomplishing one of the most sought-after superpowers: flying! To impress them, and to enroll them into your leadership authority, well that's something many would perceive to be an impossible mission.

How did Ashley practice presence to synergize with flight operations, and gain their respect? She curated a personalized experience that spoke to their values. Within weeks of starting in her new role, Ashley recognized that she needed to connect with flight operations on a personal level. She got curious about what motivated them and came up with an ingenious idea.

She reached out to Tesla and asked to host a team building event, where the pilots could experiment with their newest acceleration and auto-drive features. Pilots jumped at this opportunity and hit the gas. They tested Tesla's acceleration speed of 0 to 60 in 2.3 seconds. They swerved along empty roads to see which traffic lanes the car picked up and autocorrected. They goofed around with Tesla's inside features, chuckling each time "someone" farted from a push of a button.

Mark Grock, system chief pilot at Allegiant Airlines, described Ashley's originality and partnership as "genuine and effective."[4] He personally thanked the entire TA team for not only enhancing flight operation's internal culture, but the culture of Allegiant Airlines as a whole. Ashley won over this group by tuning into their values of speed, precision, and innovation, opening the team up to her feedback on how to better their talent acquisition and retention strategy.

As you can see, when individuals and groups appreciate learning from one another, they collaborate. Collaboration isn't a new concept in the workforce. It has always been a tool. Once Millennials entered the workforce in volume, we saw how collaboration became a driver for this generation's workforce, which reflected in our office design and workplace culture. "We" removed big offices. "We" broke down walls and created open desk concepts. "We" shifted to a culture of collaboration. "We" crashed" but "we" works! "We" derives from a culture of constructive energy and will continue to evolve into the phygital (physical and digital) as Gen Z continues to permeate the workforce.

Why is collaboration in the workplace so energizing? To start, when individuals collaborate, they bring together diverse perspectives, experiences, and knowledge. When individuals become "we," they become a pod, and start to form their own language, coming back to Skerry's orcas. Each time an idea gets bounced off another person, it continues to refine and reshape. As thoughts continue to shift and transform, energy increases, fostering an environment of psychological safety. In a psychologically safe environment, people feel comfortable to experiment, without fear of judgment or repercussions. This diversity of ideas transforms into flow, which is exactly what transpired within our team at Allegiant Airlines.

"Flow is the way people describe their state of mind when consciousness is harmoniously ordered, and they want to pursue whatever they are doing for its own sake."[5] When you experience flow, you can focus on a task without distraction. Because of your dedicated concentration, you can clearly define your goals, and put actions towards those goals. When you are experiencing flow, you approach your challenges with a balanced set of skill sets, confidently exhibiting control over your tasks which enables you to move through your challenges towards a solution. When you're in flow, time flies by. When you're in flow, you feel joy. When you're in flow, you are energized!

How many times have you noticed the day fly by when you're busy at work? I can't even count how many times I asked, "Where did the day go?" while experiencing flow with the team throughout my time at Allegiant Airlines. Challenges came our way, and we approached each challenge as an opportunity, reaping the rewards of practicing presence, collaborating, and syncing with each's energy towards creating innovative solutions.

Now that I've outlined how presence, flow, and collaboration lead to creative solutions, let's explore how this equation will impact the future of the workplace. "The U.S. Bureau of Labor Statistics projects that Gen Z will account for 30 percent of the U.S. civilian labor force by 2030."[6] As the most diverse generation, the first generation to be born with technology in-hand, and the most homeschooled generation even before the pandemic, we are entering into a new space, a phygital workplace.

"Phygital is the concept of using technology to bridge the digital world with the physical world with the purpose of providing a unique interactive experience for the user."[7] As we continue to navigate a flexible work environment with a variety of options from remote to hybrid to in-person, plus a multigenerational workplace of Boomers, Gen X, Millennials, and Gen Z, it will be more important than ever for companies to collaborate with their employees to craft curated experiences personalized to each of their employee's needs. What will the future of the workplace look like?

This past month, I worked out of a Selina in Nosara, Costa Rica, catapulting me into flow to write this and the previous chapter. "Selina provides guests with beautiful places to stay, travel, and work abroad indefinitely."[8] I went to Selina alone, not knowing anyone. As soon as I checked in, I became a "we," and collaborated with individuals from around the world. We worked in co-working offices and outdoor spaces. We explored food tastings together, nature walks, dance classes, and more. Diverse ideas were welcome and fostered unique experiences to learn from each other, which we then each infused into our corporate learnings and entrepreneurial journeys. This type of experience is the future of the workplace.

In order for us to thrive at work, the future of the workplace must mirror the same energy and personalization we put into our customer experience. As I marinated on this concept, I had an epiphany. Which industry crafts the best client experiences, energizing their customers through challenge with presence, collaboration, and flow, and mirrors our workplace demographics most closely? The fitness industry! According to a *Forbes* article,[9] the transformation of the fitness industry due to Millennials and Gen Z will continue propel the following trends forward:

- Outdoor fitness
- Remote personal training and wellness coaching
- Specialized fitness programs for risk groups
- Inclusion of mind and body fitness
- At-home in-person and remote workouts

How do these trends correlate to the workplace?

- Workplace experiences
- Personal training and wellness coaching
- Specialized workplace programs to promote diversity, equity, inclusion, and accessibility (DIEA)
- Workplace inclusion and collaboration
- At-home in-person and remote work

As you can see, the parallels are uncanny. The fitness industry is leading the charge with innovative experiences that can be our pilot to new workplace trends. We even see this in how they communicate to their customers. Check out SoulCycle's Etiquette: Respect. Joy. Love:[10]

One team.

Everyone in this studio is equal and treats each other with respect.

From the heart.

Kindness above all: Treat everyone the way you would like them to treat you.

With the pack.

We feed off the rhythm of our neighbors. If you want to do your own thing, we highly encourage that, but please don't ride in the front row.

No screens.

Leave cell phones out of the studio & dim fitness watches. If you'd like, you can leave your phone with the front desk, and we'll get you if there is an emergency.

No distractions.

We rise close and can feel each other's energy. Talking during class and overpowering smells are a major distraction for those riding around you.

All love.

High fives, positive affirmations, and hugs are almost mandatory. Show your Soul Fam some love!

Why does this sentiment feel familiar? It's familiar because it mirrors many corporate murals you've seen throughout your career. What's the differentiating factor? Personal energy! The future of the workplace must foster an environment of constructive energy, shifting our workplace culture from surviving to thriving.

Action Steps and Takeaways

Highly constructive energy energizes a person's happiness, as well as an organization's culture and success.

1. How can you practice presence as an individual to connect to your thoughts and emotions to energize actions that are in line with your values and goals?

2. How can you foster an inclusive culture of psychological safety to promote diverse perspectives and create a winning team that collaborates to create innovative solutions, or what Mihaly Csikszentmihalyi defines as an "optimal experience."[11]

3. How can your organization craft a new workplace culture that curates personalized experiences to energize your employees, increasing engagement and productivity?

Final Thoughts

In this chapter, you discovered how to cultivate environments that generate level six energy to build more innovative and engaged teams. It's important to note, as with the Curious Zone, there are very few drawbacks to constructive energy. Within the Creative Zone, when others aren't experiencing your same energetic flow, they may feel like you're in the clouds. Which honestly rings true.

When you're in the zone, it's very hard for anything to pull your focus. I personally remember receiving feedback from outside employees that they didn't feel heard or seen when they popped into our TA office. To combat this concern, I shared our team dynamics with others, and scheduled open forums for others to visit. This way, we could jive uninterrupted, and be present to others during their allotted hours. Use the lessons shared from the Creative Zone as a differentiator to energize yourself and those around you. Ultimately, the outcome from these key takeaways and action steps will showcase how you can substantially strengthen your own energy levels and your team's by getting into flow.

10

The Climax Zone

It is November 12, 2022. The Green Bay Packers are at their home stadium in Green Bay, Wisconsin, competing against the Dallas Cowboys. Ramiz Ahmed is up for the kickoff. This is his first time kicking in the NFL, and the stadium is packed, seating up to 441 football fans. Ramiz hears nothing. He is 100% focused and kicks the ball 62 yards from GB 35 to DAL 3. Throughout this neck-to-neck game, Ramiz kicks off six times, three of which go to touchbacks. The Green Bay Packers win 31 to 28.

When I asked Ramiz about his experience kicking for the NFL for the first time, he replied, "I am so dialed in out there; I don't hear anything. It's all about controlling your mind."[1] Ramiz continued to elaborate that it's hard to explain the sensation he feels, because when he is in "the zone" it's as if everything outside of his focus goes dark. It's almost like an out-of-body sensation. He strives for this sensation every kick. Each time he goes onto the field, even in practice, he is purposeful and practices like it's a real game. "I have a strict regimen, so my body and mind are primed and ready for their purpose" says Ramiz.

What Ramiz is describing is the energetic sensation of the Climax Zone. Level seven energy is the highest level of constructive energy and can only be tapped into. Many explain this feeling as having an out-of-body experience. Some feel like they are in two places at once, witnessing what they are undergoing, but also executing what's happening. Tapping into this is the most powerful energy, where one can experience and create at the same time. I like to explain this as an orgasm. Yes, a person can feel orgasmic at work.

Reaching this energetic zone takes mindfulness, practice, and purpose. Let's see how Ramiz uses all three to get into the Climax Zone. Through his recommendations, explore how you can add mindfulness, practice, and purpose into your personal and professional life to reach moments of ecstasy. These energetic hits will not only increase your own energy and the energy of those around you, but this energy is also directly linked to your happiness and satisfaction with yourself and your life.

Mindfulness

When Ramiz first joined the Green Bay Packers, he described the nerves he felt walking into his initial practice. Everything was new, and he didn't know what to expect. Like anything you start, it's understandable to feel anxious. The more time goes by, the more familiar you become, and you start to settle into a rhythm of comfort. The same holds true with big moments—moments that can change your life. How can you reach a level of comfort with something new in your life, including these life-changing moments? This level of comfort takes practice, and not just practice to practice, but targeted practice mirroring "real life" situations.

To ensure you practice the most effective way to reach these moments of elation, you must start with your mind. In Chapter 9, you discovered the energetic principle of practicing presence. Practicing presence helps you get into flow, which allows you to create and connect with yourself and others. Practicing presence is a form a mindfulness, which is defined as "the basic human ability to be fully present, aware of where we are and what we're doing, and not overly reactive or overwhelmed by what's going on around us."[2] When I asked Ramiz to share how he practices mindfulness, he excitedly outlined his relationship with wellness.

Wellness requires intentional focus, time, and energy for your thoughts, emotions, and actions. Sound familiar? It should! Throughout this book I have referred to the Energetic Self-Perception Wheel presented in Chapter 3, ensuring you can identify, understand, and choose your energy connected with each pillar and energetic zone.

"The Global Wellness Institute defines wellness as the active pursuit of activities, choices and lifestyles that lead to a state of holistic health."[3] To start learning more about how his thoughts and emotions connected to his actions and energy, Ramiz jumped into investigation mode. He led with curiosity to research health and wellness resources. He sought out doctors, coaches, and therapists. He followed social media accounts that promoted wellness and mindfulness, pulling from their recommendations to see what worked best for him. He spent time connecting with his coach to learn more about his voyage with wellness and inquired with his teammates on who they followed and recommended.

As a wellness practitioner, I loved learning about Ramiz's wellness voyage. His journey not only mirrored my own in many ways, but it brought us back to our family origins in Pakistan. I remember learning of my father's childhood, how he migrated from India to Pakistan in the late 1940s, and his lessons learned from Gandhi and Islam. While we weren't raised Muslim, and both Ramiz and I initially sought out resources through modern technology, and our excursion into wellness came full circle, connecting our past, present, and future.

Through his studies, Ramiz was introduced to the power of practicing presence through meditation. Meditation is the "profound and extended contemplation or reflection in order to achieve focused attention or an otherwise altered state of consciousness and to gain insight into oneself and the world."[4] Ramiz started consistently using the Green Bay Packers meditation room and found that practicing presence through meditation allowed him to prep for training and then game time more effectively, ensuring he was in the right mindset to get into the zone when his turn was up.

How can you use these lessons to elevate your energy levels in preparation for moments of concentration, innovation, and bliss? Even though Ramiz is an athlete, any individual can practice mindfulness through both passive and active meditation. Passive meditation is usually performed sitting down or lying in a comfortable position. Active meditation allows you to be in a meditative state even while you are performing activities such as eating, listening to music, or exercise. A variety of tools and techniques are available, from breathing exercises to guided narrations. The focus is the same: your energy is directed inwards so you can explore yourself, versus focusing on the external world.

Explore what mindfulness techniques serve you, to elevate your energy. No matter what activities you pursue to better acquaint yourself with your internal self, you will quickly experience the benefits of your practice. These benefits include reduced stress levels, allowing you to shift your energy from negative to positive so you can choose your responses to external factors versus react when you're not in control. You will experience an increase in your cognitive abilities to process information and concentrate, in both personal and professional settings. This focus directly correlates to happiness and emotional well-being in one's personal life, as well as increased satisfaction and productivity in one's professional life.

It is worth noting that the benefits of meditation may vary for each individual, and they tend to accumulate over time with consistent practice. Consistency and commitment are key to experiencing the full range of advantages that mindfulness brings, which leads us to my next recommendation: practice.

Practice

Once you've discovered what tools you want to use to exercise mindfulness, you must put these tools into action. You can research and read about anything as much as you want, but to get good at something, you must do the work. It takes most people some time to get good at something new. Yes, we've all probably had moments of glory succeeding at something our first time. You might naturally be good at attempting presence from the start. To excel and propel your energy into the Climax Zone, you must be intentional and practice effectively.

Effective practice differs by person. Ramiz accentuated how important he found mirroring his rehearsals to actual NFL games. Some players can make jokes and exchange small talk during training. Ramiz found that applying presence during football practice, emulating his energy from meditation, helped him create a routine to get into flow, with hits of level seven energy: "I set an intention for each time I train. I have a strict regimen I follow every day. I am never out there aimlessly kicking, unless that was my intention for the day, which is sometimes the case."

Each time he goes out onto the field, he does his warmup the same way. The goal of repeating his identical routine is to ensure his body and mind are primed and ready for what he's about to put it through. This way, when it's game time, his body and mind are already familiar and comfortable with the setting, because repetition builds muscle memory and automation. If nerves do start to arise, Ramiz reminds himself that he's been there before and knows what he's doing. This affirmation allows him to shift his energy from tension to familiarity.

This same structure is used in internships and training programs. Look how long it takes to become an MD. Doctors practice for years, even after receiving their bachelor's and graduating from medical school. After graduation, they continue to a one-year internship and then progress into residency, which takes an average of four and a half years. During this entire training period, they must be supervised to practice medicine.

Chad Goffstein, MD, an anesthesiologist in Las Vegas, discussed why a doctor's journey is so long, and that truly their practice never ends. According to Goffstein, "taking care of patients has always been referred to as the 'practice of medicine.' This is because medicine is an ever-changing lifelong journey, where one must not only improve the health of your individual patients, but also advance public health as a whole. This journey begins with young doctors in their internship and residency as they begin to learn they will have a life of trying to perfect their patient care, only to find out one can always practice harder."[5]

How else can practice elevate your energy? Practice sharing in other's energy! Ramiz emphasized the importance of reaching out to mentors and coaches to practice mindfulness. Because his coaches and mentors have been in his shoes before him, their insights and recommendations provide guidance and clarity. "We often forget to seek out guidance from our mentors and coaches" shares Ramiz. It's important to consistently engage in conversations, ask questions, and share your thoughts and emotions with these trusted leaders. All humans have blind spots. Mentors and coaches are just a few trained professionals who are experienced in identifying and pointing out these blind spots.

Who do you call for support to navigate challenges? Do you invest in services from a coach, mentor, therapist, and/or psychiatrist? Corporate wellness and mental health have skyrocketed in importance over the past few years. "Putting mental health at the center of workplace policies is more important than ever. . . . Extensive psychological research shows the importance of providing mental health coverage, appropriate training for employees, flexible work options, and equity in the workplace, among other evidence-based tactics to improve the workplace."[6]

Through company-sponsored wellness programs, employees have access to employee assistant programs (EAP), for mental and physical health services. Karey Larsen, a licensed professional counsel (LPC), highlighted the following: "When an individual's mental health suffers, everything in their world suffers, as work, relationships, and physical health are all interconnected. Problems don't go away. They need to be acknowledged, processed, and healed. If an employee knows their employer acknowledges the importance of taking care of their mental health and offers resources to help, they are more likely to face the struggle instead of ignoring it. This becomes a win-win for both employers and employees, amplifying the importance of humanizing the workforce."[7]

Do you know what services your organization offers to support you in your health and wellness needs? Research them. Reach out to HR. Commit to a standard schedule and sequence with these resources. Additionally, engage with trusted members of your circle to build community, ensuring you practice asking for support as much as you support yourself, and even those around you.

Practicing effectively to steadily sharpen your skills and well-being will improve your talent and abilities. Preparation, repetition, and rehearsal are essential to grow and enhance your capabilities. With time and consistency, your systemic routines will empower you to overcome limitations and break through barriers, enriching your potential. Ultimately, the better you get, the more confidence you exude, energizing you to excel in any area you choose.

Purpose

How do you know what to choose? This is where finding your purpose comes in. For the most part, the what and the how are outlined for most roles. Positions are created from a job description. To perform the duties of your role, you're provided with a plethora of resources, including policies, guidebooks, standard operating procedures (SOPs), training, and leadership guidance, to name a few. Why do you do what you do? That comes from within, and for many is the hardest question to answer.

Simon Sinek is a visionary who has dedicated his career to helping individuals find their "why." "WHY goes much deeper to understanding what motivates and inspires us. It is the purpose, cause or belief that drives every organization and every person's individual career."[8]

How do you define your purpose? Does your "why" directly connect to your career? Jack Welch, former CEO of General Electric, designed a vitality curve defining the four Es of GE leadership: "very high *energy* levels, the ability to *energize* others around common goals, the *edge* to make tough yes-and-no decisions, and finally, the ability to consistently *execute* and deliver on their promises."[9]

Based on his review of his talent pool, he defined his A players at work as "people who are filled with passion, committed to making things happen, open to ideas from anywhere, and blessed with lots of runway ahead of them. They have the ability to energize not only themselves, but everyone who comes into contact with them. They make business productive and fun at the same time." Jack's energetic vitality curve mirrors the energetic impact of constructive energy shared throughout each constructive energetic zone. He also provides a prelude to the contagious and influential power of this work (a prequel to the upcoming closing chapters).

What if you don't pursue your passion at work? Are you no longer an A player? Absolutely not! I have worked with numerous colleagues who are experts in their role, and they separate their vocation from what brings them passion. I have connected with several individuals who value security and stability and select roles that align with this value. In doing so, they use their job to support what matters to them most and follow their passions in their personal life. It's important to emphasize these distinctions, as many people enjoy the separation. Let's explore these classifications further to better understand how to reach level seven energy, whether in your personal or professional life, and how that impacts your engagement with your work.

Energy from Pursuing Your Passions Through Work

I recently visited the Clearwater Marine Aquarium in Florida, and our guide was a marine biology student who has dedicated her life to wildlife conservation. Anya exuded energy touring us through the surgery center, rehabilitation zones, feeding rooms, and even the water filtration room. Even though she has years of school before she graduates with her PhD and can perform her dream job, she's chosen roles that directly correlate to her purpose. In doing so, she is motivated and engaged to come to work to help the animals, as well as educate tourists, children, and tour groups daily.

Ramiz explained his purpose through his values. Since childhood, he loved sports. As he grew older, he learned that his values for excellence, competition, and fun all aligned with his talent for kicking. Because he's living in line with his values, he gives 100% to fulfill his drive to be an NFL kicker. "Every day I love waking up to pursue my passion for kicking for the NFL. Even when I have exhausting days, I am proud of my dedication towards excellence and always strive to be better."

When you marry your career to your purpose, an intrinsic motivation occurs, keeping you internally driven and focused. Because of this intrinsic motivation, these individuals tend to be the most engaged, highly productive, and innovative. Their energetic peaks stimulate their drive, and those around them.

Energy from Your Personal Passions

If you were born and raised in the United States, you probably notice that most people introduce themselves based on their vocation. When I moved to Salamanca, Spain, for a summer during high school, I learned this differed in other areas of the world. As students, we were taught that in Spain and throughout Europe, it may be perceived as rude to ask someone what they do for a living. Our teachers advised us that culturally, many Europeans don't define themselves by their job. They define themselves by their family, passions, hobbies, and interests, to name a few.

Pursuing your desires in your personal life can provide the same ecstasy Ramiz experiences when he kicks. As Karey emphasized, your mental health is linked to all areas of your life, not just work. Thus, if you prefer this separation and find the balance energizing, great!

If you value adventure, seek activities that challenge and excite you. You're bound to experience level seven energy exploring the unknown tastes, sights, and sounds of the world. If your value is serenity, your energetic hits may occur gardening, relaxing in your home sanctuary, or birdwatching. If your mission is to help those struggling with addiction, each person you support from their lowest low might be the link to you connecting with your highest energetic high, knowing you're saving lives. Lean into your hobbies, passions, mission, and motivators to pursue what elevates your energy to moments of paradise. Use the energy you gain from those personal drivers to continuously fuel your engagement at work.

Energy from Your "Work Family"

How else do others reach moments of bliss at work? Many obtain energy from their "work family." In Chapter 9, I shared how my pod of colleagues at Allegiant became my "work family." No matter how challenging the day was, my team not only got me through, but we also elevated each other to keep us striving towards our goals. Our presence and collaboration not only enhanced our energy to moments of innovation, but also innovated the energy around us throughout Allegiant Airlines.

If your "work family" stimulates your energy to execute your tasks, continue to use each other's constructive energy to drive forward towards your shared goals. The energetic hits you get from bouncing off each other can easily transcend to moments of elation. The experience gained from this team's flow and moments of elation will be lifelong tools to carry forward as you continue to energize yourself and those around you.

Energy from Your Personal Journey

What if you are still in pursuit of linking your passion to work, but still haven't found that perfect "Goldilocks" chair? It's understandable to feel anxiety (level one) and frustration (level two) while exploring the unknown. The unknown is unpredictable, which naturally causes fear. What if, instead of fearing this sensation, you fell in love with it? Let's look at a few examples to shift your narrative.

Destructive Thought/ Emotion	Reframed Constructive Thought/Emotion
I don't know what I want to be when I grow up. I feel lost.	I have the ability to do anything I want! I'm excited to explore the possibilities!
There are too many options. I feel overwhelmed.	Let me start by exploring opportunities of interest. The great thing is, if I don't like something, I can easily shift and pursue my next area of interest!
I haven't found anything I like.	I am getting closer to my passions, as I cross off from my list the interests that don't inspire me.

One of the best pieces of advice I received when I transitioned from the corporate world to being an entrepreneur was that I needed to redefine failure. I was seeking a challenge and growth. Challenge and growth come with growing pains. Remember that switch I spoke about in Chapter 6 within the Compromise Zone? When you compromise on your desires to avoid pain, you also avoid everything that you could gain. The Climax Zone is that gain. The feeling of elation you experience within this energy is wonderful and invigorating. Bask in those moments. You will need that energy as you strive towards your goals.

If I didn't fail every day, if I didn't feel uncomfortable every day, that meant I wasn't growing. The fear and discomfort I still feel every day fuel me with energy and excitement. I've reframed my uneasiness with entrepreneurship, similar to how I've reframed my "love" for green juice in the morning. It's now become a craving I can't live without yet still don't like to taste. This is why it's so important to be present though your journey. When you are present to the growth you are experiencing, innovative hits will come through. These hits of revelation are level seven energy and will bring you the clarity and direction you seek towards your goals and dreams. How so?

When you're starting out, you may not know what you're passionate about. If you jumped into a role when you were younger and continued that path without question, you may be asking yourself the same question much later in your career. Wherever you are, you can always choose to make a change. Your past is not a waste of energy. There are always takeaways you can use to design your desired future, starting with your values.

After hearing Brian Skerry's story on "The Secret Culture of Killer Whales" podcast,[10] I had to reach out! Skerry shared that his journey started out as a child. "I was very interested in exploration. And that always energized me . . . the idea of discovery . . . it's very powerful, almost an aphrodisiac, where you just get addicted to the notion of exploration and discovery."[11] Skerry's curiosity for discovery led him to dive into stone quarries, which also led him to building a lucrative business removing and selling car parts found in these quarries. By being present to his value of exploration and curiosity, Skerry started to pick up any diving job that came his way, including shipwrecks and German U-boats in the North Atlantic!

In 2021, Skerry won an Emmy Award for Outstanding Documentary or Nonfiction Series for "Secrets of the Whales." As you can see, his journey started with a value, and led him to a passionate career. And his journey continues. "It's been a lifelong journey . . . and along the way, a lot of things happened that I couldn't have ever predicted. One of those was that I began to see a lot of problems in the world's oceans." As a journalist, Skerry is now "energized by the potential to shine a light on some of these big problems and look for solutions." He explained, "I get energized by knowing that there's another generation out there who needs that sort of information and inspiration, and to the degree that I can help with that to some small part, then then that's what I want to do."

Skerry's story is just one of millions that started with a value and continued onto a successful dream. Take his story and start with your values. What positions and interests align with your values? If you value family, you might want to look for roles that allow you to either work with families or offer work-life harmony, so you have plenty of time with your own family. If you value communication, seek out roles that align with your desired method of communication. Even if you end up not liking a job you started, at least you now know you can remove that role from your list of interests.

Take the lessons shared in the "Mindfulness," "Practice," and "Purpose" sections earlier in this chapter about mindset and presence and apply them to your search for purpose. Sometimes it's just a numbers game. Set your intention to discover your passions. Leverage mindfulness to be diligent throughout your discovery. Success is discovered through failures every day. Nothing is discovered when you don't try.

Action Steps and Takeaways

What are three ways to reach the Climax Zone?

1. Mindfulness
2. Practice
3. Purpose

What is one action you can take to practice mindfulness?

_____

_____

_____

How can you improve your practice to enhance your skill set?

_____

_____

_____

How do your passions energize your purpose?

_____

_____

_____

How can your values help you find your "dream" job?

_____

_____

_____

Final Thoughts

Now that you have completed Chapter 10, you have a full comprehension of all seven levels of energy. You now can decipher your core thoughts, emotions, and actions and align them with each energetic zone. As you experience higher levels of energy, your approach to situations in your day-to-day and under stress will become easier, more enjoyable, and more energizing. Continue to practice, be present, and strive towards your purpose. In doing so, you can reach continuous hits of ecstasy, providing clarity and moments of brilliance. The chapter key takeaways and actions steps provide you with the tools to make shifts in your personal energy to enhance how you're experiencing life in your professional and personal life.

CHAPTER

11

How to Shift Your Energy

Where focus goes, energy flows.

—Tony Robbins[1]

Now that you have been given the foundation for each energy zone, I am going to take you on a journey empowering your choices, so you too can create solutions to any challenge you face. I'll do so by sharing examples focusing on five energetic success principles:

1. The Principle of Detachment
2. Practice Presence
3. Create Possibility
4. Cultivate Curiosity
5. Lead with Love (or Care)

These principles have demonstrated success with thousands of individuals, teams, and companies worldwide. With practice, you too will discover how you can shift your own energy. From there, you can use these same tools and principles and extend them outwards, shifting the energy of those around you.

The Principle of Detachment

When I received a referral introduction to Nicole, a USC Gould School of Law graduate, I looked forward to connecting with her to better understand her goals and desires. At the time, Nicole was a personal stylist, running her own small business. She graduated top of her class from law school and had attempted to pass the State Bar of California twice, without success. She pivoted and leaned into another one of her passions, fashion, using her law degree to assist her in setting up her own LLC and contracts with clients.

After three successful years as a personal stylist, she received an offer to sell her company, providing an opportunity for her to strategize her next move. Within her first month of coaching, Nicole gained clarity on her values and vision. She quickly realized that she still had a thirst for pursuing a career as an attorney. The challenge was that, when it came to passing the State Bar of California, she had attached that vision of herself to failure. She had excelled in law school and knew she understood the material, but she felt such anxiety when it came to test taking that she burst into a panic attack even when simply describing her emotions (level one).

As we progressed with our coaching engagements, Nicole continued to work on her mindset. I knew passing the test wasn't going to be the hard part. I needed to shift her mindset and energy and coach her on how to detach from her failed vision of herself. Nicole started meditating, creating vision boards of what she looked like as the in-house counsel at a company. Naturally, her vision board attorney outfits were fabulous!

As we continued our work together, Nicole started recognizing her inner critic, and began to disassociate with its messages. To do this, rather than empowering those voices in your head, thank them for keeping you safe. From there, tell them you are in control of making choices that best serve and energize you. We are all unique individuals, so how you name your inner critic and how you communicate with those voices will differ from someone else's. The takeaways are that it's imperative you recognize when you're experiencing doubt and label those emotions and thoughts. From there you can then take time to breathe, giving you the space to recognize your current level of energy, and then decide what level of energy you want to choose moving forward. For Nicole—a former dancer—this meant doing a pirouette each time a destructive thought came in. The physical movement flowing through her doubt brought a smile to her face, causing her energy to shift. The symbolism of twirling out of destructive to constructive energy was beautiful for me to witness as a coach.

Once Nicole was able to envision herself as a successful attorney, we strategized learning techniques and altered her entire method of studying. As many do, Nicole attached herself to the pain she experienced in her past. It's as if her mindset traveled back in time to the rigor of law school, reexperiencing the dreaded hours of drowning herself in books. Why does something you want to accomplish have to be so painful? It doesn't! Once again, this was a narrative from her past. To shift her energy, we focused on building constructive energy, celebrating after she completed each round of flashcards. Nicole's perspective of studying transformed from pain to gain, and she flew through her preparation materials in less than four months.

Nicole approached the State Bar of California with excitement and determination, passing with ease (level six). Based on her past internships and success in school, she was offered an in-house counsel job at her employer of choice, and even created a mentorship program for law students, sharing her success story and alternative approach to becoming an attorney.

The principle of detachment allows you to disconnect from whatever is holding you back, and whatever is out of your control. In this example, Nicole had attached herself to failure when it came to being an attorney. The story she told herself became her truth, which is a limiting belief. By detaching from the limiting narrative she had linked herself to, she was able to choose her own narrative, one that aligned with her vision, values, and goals.

How can you put this into practice? Every time you catch yourself in a limiting belief, separate out your facts and fiction. Let's walk through this exercise together. What were the facts in this instance? What were the stories Nicole told herself?

Fact 1: Nicole graduated top of her class from law school.

Fact 2: Nicole failed the State Bar of California twice.

Story 1: Nicole was a failure and couldn't pass the State Bar of California.

Story 2: Nicole couldn't pursue her dream to become an attorney.

When you distinctly separate fact from fiction, it's clear how much you've attached yourself to a narrative of self-doubt and fear (level one). By performing this application, you can highlight your limiting beliefs and reframe your narrative to what you choose and design a path forward to accomplish your chosen future.

What are some other ways we can use the principle of detachment? In Chapter 7, I showcased the power of detaching from others' destructive energy. If you encounter negative energy while you're interacting with someone, it's compassionate to empathize with them and see the world through their lens, so they feel heard and understood (level four). It's also just as important to detach from their energy, because their storyline and experience are not yours to wear. I like to visualize this like taking off someone else's coat. If the act of removing an invisible coat of negative energy helps you perform the detachment, the way the pirouette helped Nicole shift her energy, lean into the action.

The final recommendation under the principle of detachment we also explored in Chapter 7 and Chapter 8 is the importance of detaching from your own solutions when you are helping someone else through their challenges. When I recounted my energy at the close of PNK, it's easy to see why I was so exhausted by the end of the day. In addition to wearing my team member's energy, I was attached to each team member's outcome. At present, I coach and consult clients for hours on end, yet never hit that lower level of energy I used to experience. Why? Because I apply the principle of detachment.

It's important to remember that we are diverse human beings with various intersectionalities. Just because something worked for you doesn't mean it will work for someone else. Yes, you can share your experiences and leave room for others to choose to follow your path if the path you took works best for them. But the most powerful way to coach someone is to respond with a question instead of an answer. When you respond with questions instead of answers to help guide a person to their own solution, you will gain energy from assisting them, and see them find their own journey to success.

Practice Presence

Early in 2023, I was asked to take lead as a consultant for the Department of Defense Education Activity (DoDEA). Mr. Barry Thomas had been leading diversity, equity, and inclusion (DEI) project work with DoDEA for the past year and a half, coming from more than 20 years as an industry leader. Barry received an offer to return to the education sector as vice president of Community Engagement for Teach for America. I couldn't have been more excited for him and his next adventure, as he continued to be a DEI provocateur in educational leadership.

At the time, I had extensive experience with DEI project work and consulting. My expertise within universities and graduate schools was also comprehensive. However, my knowledge of federally operated school systems was limited. To get up to speed, I shadowed and partnered on assignments, strategies, and training, to ensure the transition would be as seamless as possible.

When you start a new role, it's easy to jump into task mode. Most people love to take notes, outline resources, and build checklists. In a professional learning series virtual session, Barry reminded me of the power of practicing presence. When you focus and tune into the task at hand, free of distractions, your energy elevates into a flow (level six), allowing you to learn from a 360-degree view. In this session, Barry shared an example of how practicing presence can shift perspectives and open lines of communication.

Before consulting for DoDEA, Barry was the director of equity and diversity for Omaha Public Schools in Nebraska. Part of his role consisted of observing and evaluating public school standards and best instructional practices, to ensure each school met the requirements to maintain their accreditation. As part of the accreditation process, each school developed a portfolio, detailing their policies, procedures, practices, and supporting data. The final piece of maintaining one's accreditation was on-site observations.

It was the middle of winter in Omaha when Barry and his colleagues visited a local elementary school for on-site observations. He and his team arrived early to ensure they all received their agenda for the day and had time to introduce themselves to the teachers they would be shadowing. Teachers were prepped for observations and had lesson plans outlined to showcase student engagement and best instructional practices.

After the team met, Barry approached the outside entrance of the school, observing students being welcomed by teachers as they entered the building. As Barry was monitoring student-teacher interactions, he noticed a young man walking up the sidewalk with his hoodie on under his winter jacket. As this young man arrived at school, he was immediately approached by a teacher, asking him to take off his hoodie. The teacher didn't welcome the student by name or greet the student with a good morning salutation. The student continued walking up the sidewalk to the main entrance, ignoring the teacher.

Within seconds, another teacher approached the student and asked him to take off his hoodie. Again, this student wasn't welcomed by name, or provided a good morning salutation. Once again, the student continued walking up the sidewalk into the building, ignoring the second request. As the student was about to enter the building, a third teacher repeated the command, demanding the student acknowledge the directive. They didn't provide an explanation as to why this request was so important; they just mirrored the last two commands. The student continued to ignore the requests and entered the building. While doing so, Barry watched these three teachers throw up their arms in frustration, acknowledging each other's actions, shaking their heads.

After witnessing these three exchanges, Barry was intrigued. Why was this student defiant? Curious, he followed the student into the building, immediately noticing that the student was walking toward the other end of the hallway, back outside. As he continued to follow the student outside, Barry greeted the student, and then introduced himself. He shared why he was visiting the school, and asked the young man if he wouldn't mind answering a question for him.

The student agreed, and Barry said that he was present upon the student's arrival and witnessed three teachers asking him to remove his hoodie. He shared that he also noticed the young man didn't comply, and wondered why. The student explained that he had just walked from his house to school on this frigid winter day. His head and ears were freezing. He then also said that his class was outside in a trailer. Because he knew he was just walking in and out of the main door entrance to the outside trailers, it didn't make sense to remove his hoodie to go right back outside into the cold. Barry thanked the young man for explaining his reaction and wished him a good day of school.

By practicing presence, Barry gained an additional perspective and opened lines of communication with this young man. Behavior that was perceived noncompliant was actually completely understandable. Barry pointed out that these interactions could have become very destructive. Who knows how long this young man walked to school. If he had had a hard morning and responded negatively to the authoritarian commands, he would have received the discipline for his response, rather than the teachers for their lack of awareness about the situation.

Barry reminded everyone of the power of being present, and how presence can allow you to "take time to find the humanity in others."[2] When we "get into a routine of systems dictating behavior," we forget that there is a human behind an action. The teachers didn't welcome the student before dictating commands. If they had been present and welcoming, creating a safe space for this young man as he entered school, he might have responded differently. Additionally, these teachers didn't ask why this young man was wearing a hoodie. They didn't explain why the policy existed. All of these were missed opportunities to open communication and be present with their student.

Practicing presence takes practice! Our brains aren't wired to process as much as information as what is constantly coming at us . Therefore, it takes focus and repetition. To enhance this skill, separate the various ways you want to practice presence, so you can concentrate on each, one at a time.

Some examples of ways you can practice presence include meditation, practicing presence with your inner thoughts. You can practice presence with listening, masking your sight to enhance your auditory skills. You can also focus on sight, becoming deaf to your surroundings to fine-tune your vision.

How present are you with your colleagues? Do you catch yourself multitasking in meetings? If so, practice presence by removing distractions so you can focus all your energy and attention on the meeting deliverables and attendees. How present are you with your family and friends? Do you find yourself providing input before they are done speaking? Practice active listening to ensure you are attentively listening to what others are asking of you. They may just want a sounding board rather than advice. Do you tend to scroll through your social media, rather than communicating with those around you? Allocate time to scroll through social media when you are alone, so you can focus on having fruitful conversations and interactions with others when you're in their company. However you decide to practice presence, remember to give yourself grace, and realize this skill will never be a check-the-box accomplishment. Practicing presence will be a lifetime of work that will continuously evolve as humanity evolves.

Create Possibility

In 2023, I was the keynote speaker for the annual event of the Healthcare Financial Management Association (HFMA), San

Diego chapter. Aaron Crane, HFMA national chair, announced that the theme was "Ignite the Spark." The healthcare industry was experiencing very high rates of burnout, turnover, and healthcare inequities. I was hired to shift the San Diego chapter's group of about 250 healthcare finance leaders from destructive to constructive energy, empowering HFMA's message. "The pandemic and the challenges of the last few years has made us stronger, teaching us as leaders to tap into our strength, stand tall face our issues head on and remain flexible to adapt to change. Nothing is impossible. We are inspired to keep finding ways to 'IGNITE THE SPARK' to keep yourself challenged and the folks that you lead around you engaged. This theme is something we all need to embrace."[3]

The evening prior to the conference, I happened to connect with a few attendees at the Rancho Bernardo Inn lobby restaurant, where I introduced myself as their keynote, and inquired a bit about their roles. These attendees shared specifics about some of their challenges as well as insights on workshops they were eager to attend the next day. Their energy was enthusiastic; they were motivated to learn more about my keynote message and were hopeful for an energetic shift from the conference as a whole.

In hearing our animated discussion, another group of attendees also approached, energized to connect with industry colleagues they recognized from other hospitals. Amid the chatter and connections, I asked a simple question. I don't actually remember what prompted me to ask it, but it became the question that shifted BoBae, an assistant controller, to create a possibility she didn't believe existed. What question did I ask that led to BoBae's transformation? "What do you want?"

BoBae was in her 50s and had worked her way up through finance and accounting for 31 years. She was loyal to her employer, staying with her present company for the last 13 years. She was recently promoted to lead a new team as her organization created standardized processes across their various locations. When she accepted the role, she knew that there would be challenges, because this role and department, in the structure presented, was a completely new approach for her organization.

When I started working with BoBae, she had been in her role for about nine months and was exhausted. When I connected with her via Zoom, I could see how she was carrying that exhaustion. Her eyes were puffy from crying and not sleeping, her shoulders were hunched over, revealing her deflation, and her hands were shaking in fear (level one). Our bodies tell us when we are experiencing a values misalignment. It's up to us to acknowledge their retaliation and make changes to move forward with constructive energy. I consoled BoBae and asked her to walk me through her current situation.

BoBae shared that she felt alone. She oversaw a new department but didn't have any guidance from leadership on how to navigate the specifics. Each time she hired talent to grow the department, they left within 90 days, at best, stating the workload was not sustainable. To combat the month-end fatigue that was causing this attrition, BoBae worked weekends and evenings. She didn't want to place month-end closing requirements on her team, fearful the members she inherited would walk too.

BoBae explained that the one question I asked, "What do you want?" ignited a spark deep within her. After experiencing my keynote the following morning, she leaned into the "Ignite the Spark" message. Could it actually be possible to change your life in your 50s? She said she really didn't believe anything could change so late in the game, but it was worth a consultation to see how coaching could better her current personal and professional life.

Most take time to reflect on their values, and each client has their own version of an epiphany when asked to complete this exercise. BoBae's journey mirrored the same voyage I see with many women I coach. She couldn't believe how hard it was to answer questions about herself. Her wants? Her desires? Her values? She had always put everyone around her first.

I validated BoBae's experience, as many women epitomized her same generational and cultural expectations. For all you self-identifying females: How many times throughout your childhood were you told to be a good little girl? "Follow the rules." "Respect your elders." "Be a good helper." The message she received was different from the message her brothers received. We all know the saying "Boys will be boys!" When she asked her brothers the same question, "What do you want?" they all immediately answered without hesitation. They laughed together when they discussed this, as BoBae's mom validated that each time the boys screamed and threw a temper tantrum, she naturally asked, "What do you want" to stop the ruckus. Anytime BoBae acted up, her mother's reaction was one of discipline and disappointment: she was a lady and should know better.

This is why BoBae, and many more of my female clients, have such a hard time answering questions like "What do you want?" This was the first time someone truly asked her that question, and she's in her 50s! It's no wonder that one little question I asked at HFMA completely changed her life. Once BoBae got clear on her values, it was time to energize those values. The challenge was that BoBae was experiencing a block about answering that infamous question.

To overcome this challenge, I mirrored a technique I shared earlier. Name your gremlins to disassociate yourself from your inner critic. In parallel, I had BoBae name her inner cheerleader. She named her Limitless because she didn't want her to experience the same limits she had always put on herself. Anything was possible for Limitless! Coming from that perspective, BoBae and I started to ask, "What does Limitless want?"

Desire 1: Body Image

Limitless wanted her body back. How could she create that possibility for Limitless? BoBae hired a trainer and nutritionist to realign her actions with her value of health and wellness. Over the previous nine months, BoBae had gained 15 pounds, too exhausted to cook and work out (level one). Limitless prioritized her trainer. Her workouts energized her midday, so she could return to work with energy to work the extra hours into the evening (level four, level six). As shared in Chapter 7, it's imperative that you add energetic recharges throughout your day, similar to how you charge your phone when your battery is low. If you don't plug in, your battery will empty, causing you to shut down.

Desire 2: Work-Life Harmony

BoBae divulged that she had disconnected from spending quality time with her husband and children for the past six months, returning home late from work, too exhausted to engage in thoughtful conversations or family activities (level one). Weekends were even worse. If she worked, her routine stayed the same as it was during the week. If she didn't, she stayed in bed, catching up on the sleep she needed from long hours during the week (level one). Family was one of her values, and she missed the energy she used to get from their connection.

How could she possibly reconnect Limitless with her family, when she had been so distant for so long? Limitless loved to cook. Healthy food fueled her energy. Limitless also loved to laugh and dance (level four, level six, level seven). To streamline her needs and time, BoBae started by asking her family to meal prep with her twice a week. These hours of meal prep became something the entire family looked forward to. They laughed, they danced, and they shared details about their week, reconnecting them on an intimate level. BoBae started coming to our weekly sessions with excitement (level six). She thought her family would be frustrated or annoyed at her. But instead, they empathized with her work struggles and cheered her on for reconnecting with her health and loved ones, something she hadn't thought was possible!

Desire 3: Passion and Purpose

Limitless wanted to fall back in love with her job. She craved learning from others as much as she loved leading a team. She wanted to feel passionate and proud of her work. She also wanted work to be work, not her entire life. Would it be possible to start over at 50? BoBae always wanted to explore other industries but didn't think her experience would translate.

How could Limitless find out if her skills were transferable? Limitless would share her experience with others and ask. She wasn't fearful of feedback. She was excited to learn and grow. What do you think happened as soon as BoBae shared her experience at a friend's pool party the following weekend? She received a call from a CEO, asking to discuss a controller role in the entertainment industry. This CEO shared that she loved her diverse background and values, and this role would also grow into a CFO role, because the current CFO had announced he would retire in two years and was looking to grow a person into his current position. In less than one month, BoBae had a job offer honoring her values and worth—a job she never believed was possible.

By the end of our time working together, BoBae and Limitless became one. BoBae no longer feared vocalizing her wants and needs. She laughed, exclaiming, "I didn't realize how vocal I could be expressing what I want! I surprise myself now; my wants and desires just roll off my tongue!" What wasn't possible before became possible.

When you feel stuck, use this energetic principle to break down your list of "not possibles." Once you outline everything you don't believe to be possible, write down the opposite, creating the possibility. It's important to note that your list of possible outcomes can also be action verbs. BoBae aligned with listing her possibilities as nouns. She wanted a fit body. She wanted to be what she described as a fun-loving mom and wife. She wanted a career she felt passionate about and in which she could continuously learn. She could have also broken this down as creating the possibility of health and wellness, stepping into the possibility of love and fun, leading her career with the possibility of passion and growth.

Choose to create your possibilities so that they best align with your desired vision of yourself. The possibility might seem overwhelming at first, but once you develop your list of opposites, you now have a starting point and an ending point. From there you can design a step-by-step action plan to get from point A to point B. And if you need to disassociate with your cheerleader, in addition to your inner critics, explore how the example above can empower you to use your voice and communicate your worth. Step by step, you will build confidence to know your value and publicize your desires.

Cultivate Curiosity

In 2013, the Cosmopolitan of Las Vegas (TCOLV) hosted its first summer rotational internship program, totaling 10 students from universities across the United States. Not only did this intern group get to rotate through a variety of departments of interest, including resort operations, casino operations, finance, HR, customer service, and entertainment, but they also got to stay on site at the newest and one of the hottest hotels on the Las

Vegas strip. We housed interns two to a room and gave them a wraparound suite as their community quarters, with unlimited access to Co* Dining, our employee dining room that offered "a continuously changing selection of handcrafted meals daily."[4]

Over the years, I've stayed in touch with a multitude of interns from my time at TCOLV for a variety of celebratory reasons. Katie Gorski and Courtney Callan returned to TCOLV post-graduation, embarking upon careers in resort operations and banquets. I was proud to give Keith Wargula glowing reviews upon graduation, cheering him on as he landed a role with Hello! Destination Management. I remember how excited I was when Mikael Arutunian reached out to me in 2018, sharing the energy he felt giving a CapitalSpeaks speech, which mirrors the format of a TEDx Talk internally at Capital Group. In 2020, I reveled in joy hearing from Ethan Wehner, thanking me for my leadership and inspiration to follow his passion of acting, coming from a strong career in business development.

This time, I wanted to share the success of their work and accomplishments. As part of the financial services rotation, a neglected side project developed into a huge success story. The 2013 summer rotational internship program was the reason for this success. In line with our brand and talent acquisition strategy, we recruited a "curious class" of interns for cultivating curiosity to reconcile over a million dollars for resort operations. How did TCOLV define the curious class? "It's not so much a demographic. It's more of a shared attitude, so it defies ages and locations and incomes. But it's a general open-mindedness. People that are creative, like new ideas, like to travel, try new restaurants—it's that innate explorer,"[5] Marchese said. How did a group of college interns cultivate curiosity, and use it to reconcile over a million dollars for TCOLV?

In the summer of 2013, the director of finance and accounting, Victoria (Tori) Stamm, led the finance rotation. The TCOLV was in its early years of operations, and every penny counted. When the rotational internship program rotated through Tori's department, most assumed they would be crunching numbers behind a computer, enthusiastic to see how an operation of this size functioned. Tori, being the creative leader she was, had a different idea.

Each month, over $100,000 was going to "unreconciled," hitting the resort operations books as a loss. Tori didn't know why but wasn't able to prioritize and allocate resources to investigate this concern at that moment. When the 2013 summer rotational internship program got approved to include finance and accounting, the perfect marriage of opportunity occurred. She walked through the balance sheets with the team and gave them a brief overview of her understanding of the concern. Resort operations was taking a hit from the minibar, and she didn't know why. She gave the team free rein to follow their leads. And the team took on this challenge with excitement. How often are you given a problem and the freedom to fully investigate without a deadline or expectation on your back (level five and level six)? This is when the 2013 summer rotational interns, in partnership with resort operations, minibar operations, finance, and accounting, put on their investigator hats and cultivated curiosity (level five).

Many of the rotational interns had already completed a rotation in resort operations and were well versed in using the Agilyis Lodging Management System (LMS), which is one of the reasons they believed Tori aligned them with the project in the first place. Finance wasn't well versed in using the front end of LMS, because their work derived from numbers that reported out through the system. Because of the rotational internships' front-end experience with LMS, they were able to craft a list of roles that were directly connected to the minibar, reviewing the notes within the LMS of everyone who entered a room and could potentially be touching minibar items.

The team went on a fact-finding mission, interviewing housekeeping, minibar, maintenance, and the minibar vendor, Bartech. TCOLV was one of the first hotels to lead with technology in a variety of their operations, and Bartech was the vendor they used to automate the minibar in each guest room. If a hotel guest picked up an item from the minibar for more than about 60 seconds, it auto charged the guest folio to ensure they were invoiced for the items they consumed.

Through this fact-finding mission, the team learned that the only piece of the minibar operation that was automated was the 60-second removal and charge to the folio. Bartech was developing an app to ensure items could be validated live, but this app didn't exist at the time. Therefore, if a guest returned the item after 60 seconds, and stated this at checkout, the front desk would move the charge over to "unreconciled," never verifying if the item in fact had been returned.

When the team asked to bounce these records off the minibar logs, they received banker box after banker box of manual records. There was no way someone was going to go through these boxes each time to verify an item later. And due to the sheer volume of guests checking in and checking out every day at TCOLV, it didn't make sense to have someone running around room to room each time a minibar item was questioned at checkout.

To better understand how items went missing, the team selected a sample of about 30 rooms and investigated each room's activity, monitoring down to the minute each time an item was moved, and who was in the room. The team's energy was electrifying! They were having a blast investigating this mystery (level six and level seven).

After weeks of scrutinizing minibar activities, the team reported that around 80% of the minibar items allocated to "unreconciled" were still in inventory. From the sample they examined, less than 5% was a misrepresentation from guests, leaving about 15% of the minibar items being consumed by employees. From there, they provided recommendations to rectify the situation.

Recommendation 1

In reviewing the employee handbook and training protocols for employees entering the guest room, we confirmed there was no policy in place that explicitly stated that consuming an item from the minibar was classified as theft, outlining the repercussions for such actions. HR partnered with the various departments this pertained to, and ensured all employees understood the new policy and signed off on the new understanding.

Recommendation 2

Signage was placed in each guestroom at the minibar stating the process and time constraints for picking up an item. This way, guests knew if they wanted to review an item to enjoy, they only had 60 seconds to examine the item and return it, without being charged. The sign also outlined the process if they accidentally forgot to return it to its sensor within 60 seconds so they could proactively notify the front desk to ensure the charge was corrected versus being moved to "unreconciled" at checkout.

Recommendation 3

While TCOLV waited for the Bartech app to be released, TCOLV outlined a verification process if a guest stated they didn't consume an item at checkout. This way, guests knew their concern was being investigated, and they would receive a follow-up verifying the items and charges accordingly.

Because of the 2013 summer rotational internship's success, various interns were extended an opportunity to stay after completion of their summer rotational internship program. The value they brought as the first round of interns set the bar for future interns. And for most, cultivating curiosity at TCOLV was just the beginning. Since their time as interns, each has leveraged the energetic success principle of cultivating curiosity to save their current organizations hundreds of hours and millions of dollars in their various roles. This is the power of the energy of success.

Lead with Love

"Rebecca, I just feel like such a loser. I have been trying for years to be a successful real estate agent, but I've constantly failed. I had energy and passion for real estate right after I got my license. I loved being a sponge and learning about the industry from leaders at my brokerage. But within months, my husband and I found out we were pregnant, and all my energy shifted towards my first child.

"I'm so thankful for the time I got to prep for my first pregnancy and all the time little Jamar and I got to spend together during our first year. I wouldn't take that back for anything! Once Jamar turned one, I jump-started my career again and joined a new brokerage. I was so eager and truly thought I would be great at helping new moms find their first family home, just like me and my family. I started passing my card around at our country club and mommy-and-me networking events.

"But again, within months, my husband and I got pregnant. And then again! Needless to say, we're officially a family of five. But once again, I put my career on hold and focused on our beautiful family. I have been nonstop in baby mode and can't believe it's already been five years since I truly focused and worked. Yes, I've helped friends and family with real estate here and there, but I haven't had the time or energy to focus on much outside of my family. Thankfully, my oldest is now going into kindergarten, and the younger two are in preschool and daycare. I finally feel like I have the time to breathe and reflect.

"My husband makes good money, but we have credit card debt. I know the cost of schools and activities won't be sustainable for much longer if I don't go back to work. I even mustered up the courage to ask one of my dearest friends if I could help with their business. I know she could easily afford me, and I offered to do anything from retail to housekeeping. I felt snubbed because she totally dismissed me, as if I'm not worth anything. I just want to support my family; I can't believe she won't even give me a chance."

"My dear client Keysha. Thank you so much for allowing me to share your story. I remember how frustrated you were at this point in your life. And it was understandable. You didn't know your worth professionally, and you were fearful for your family, your number one value."

If Keysha's story sounds like you, I want you to take a deep breath in, deep breath out, and learn from this energetic success principle. In this chapter, I am going to outline how Keysha applied the principle of leading with love to shift her energy from destruction to construction.

At this point in Keysha's life, she was calling herself a loser and was angry at herself for not providing for her family (level one and level two). When you're calling yourself names, you are reinforcing that energy into your presence. Words matter. There are very few times when I contest a client speaking. This called for me to pull out my bullshit button, so Keysha could hear how many times she was putting herself down. Each time she did, I called bullshit, asking her to rephrase. By calling Keysha out each time she misspoke, she was able to consciously focus her energy on updating her language. Before this was brought to the forefront, she wasn't even consciously aware of how poorly she was treating herself.

Since Keysha was clear on her values and felt confident that she was living in line with her values in her personal life, we focused on her career and professional goals. I asked Keysha, "How does your career choice align with your values?" Keysha joined the real estate industry to find homes for families. The energy she exuded describing the moment a family walks into a house, visualizing holidays, celebrations, and family dinners, brought me back to my first childhood home. She had a passion, vision, and energy for making families' dream homes come true (level five, level six, and level seven).

Keysha loved the hunt to find the perfect home and welcomed the challenge the real estate industry offered. Because real estate allows you to be an independent contractor, success is directly correlated to input. When she wanted to take time off, she was her own boss, allowing her flexibility to be with her family at important events, school functions, and family vacations.

But the best part, her level seven energy, was when she watched a family step into their dream home. Yes, she loved closing a deal, but the day a family invited her family over for their home-warming party, this was the day she lit up. She just glowed sharing these moments (level six and level seven).

After having Keysha go through each value, she clearly saw that picking up odds and ends at her family friend's hotel was not in alignment with her values. If her friend had accepted her offer, that would have depleted her energy, pulling her further away from living life in alignment with what mattered to her most. Her first step in leading with love was apologizing to her dear friend, thanking her for declining her offer.

After Keysha apologized to her friend and got clear on everything she loved about real estate, it was time to better understand what was holding her back from success. What did she not love? Keysha made a list of items she didn't love doing, which ultimately fell into two buckets: marketing and administration.

Marketing

First I asked, "Keysha, what is holding you back from marketing yourself and your business?" Keysha had an energetic shift here immediately. She only self-identified as a mother and wife. When people asked her about herself, she never introduced herself as a real estate agent. Why? It's natural to share your successes. How many times have you proudly shared where you aren't succeeding? Wife and mother were the two identities Keysha associated with success.

With that understanding, I asked Keysha to vocalize how she would describe a successful real estate agent. When she outlined what success in real estate meant to her, she outlined the following items:

1. A successful real estate agent was in good standing with their license and worked for a reputable brokerage.

2. Realtors were known for trying to close deals without caring about the family's needs. Success meant people trusted their agent with their budget, desires, and family. They had a good reputation.

3. Success = $100,000 annually to start.

By breaking down these success factors, I was then able to ask Keysha where she was succeeding with each and where she was failing. She was succeeding with two out of three of these factors.

She just hadn't shared her success, which I knew would get her to number 3 quite quickly.

How could Keysha market herself and ensure people knew about her professional goals and passion for finding families a home? Keysha needed to fall in love with sharing her enthusiasm for work, just as much as her love for her family. She didn't look at her role as someone in sales. She wanted to ensure her clients knew she would honor her promise and find them their dream home. Keysha partnered with her brokerage and developed a promise statement, which is a brief sentence that sums up what you do, your target audience, and your promised outcomes to your clients. Keysha was a real estate agent who promised to find families their dream home.

In a matter of weeks after finessing her promise statement, Keysha accomplished this:

1. She started passing out business cards to her favorite restaurants, country clubs, family functions, and social events around town. She fell in love with sharing her promise, knowing her worth.

2. She leveraged an intern to create social media pages with reels highlighting homes and families she had serviced over the years. Her differentiating factor highlighted how happy these families were in their homes. The videos and pictures didn't just show staged empty bedrooms. They showed what it looked like to live in them and raise a family, messy playroom and all! Keysha fell in love telling these family's stories, and how their homes were the center of their ability to create memories for years to come.

3. She hosted an event welcoming all newcomers at the start of the school year. Glenview was growing, and she knew connecting

with newcomers from the beginning was important to ensure these families felt welcomed and had friends and resources from the get-go, building an inclusive environment.

Administration

Once Keysha felt comfortable marketing herself, she knew her list of to-dos on the admin side would increase. This list ranged from inputting new clients into the brokerage's CRM, to following up with clients after networking events and open houses, to reaching out and partnering with local services that supported everything that connected to a family's home. The more lenders, handymen, landscapers, title companies, and so on who knew she was looking for business, the more referrals could come her way.

How much does an administrative assistant make on an hourly basis in the Chicago area? Based on market data, we calculated that Keysha could hire an administrative assistant on a part-time basis to start between $17 and $25 an hour. When I had first asked Keysha what ways she could ensure administrative tasks could get completed, her energy immediately fell to the safety zone (level one). She didn't believe she had enough work for an admin to stay busy and was fearful of losing money to an unsuccessful business. #bullshit #rephrase

After receiving positive leads from her marketing efforts, Keysha knew it was imperative that she invest in her long-term success. She fell in love with finding an administrative assistant, reframing this role as an asset to growing her business. Within three months of hiring her admin, she was able to promote her to full-time status. In addition to the administrative support, Keysha discovered collaborating with her admin brought her energy. Their synergy (level six) led to innovative approaches and efficient processes.

In less than nine months, Keysha had fallen back in love with herself, her career path, her friend, and even her family. She loved how much her life changed in such a short time. She cleared $150,000 in those nine months, surpassing her annual goal under her allotted timeframe. Her efforts paid down their credit card debt, relieving her husband of the stress he previously carried as the sole income provider of the household. And even better, she was having fun. The joyousness she exuded when she found a family a home was climax energy, exclaiming each time she had an out-of-body experience, elated with energy (level seven).

As you can see though Keysha's journey, the principle of leading with love starts with loving yourself. How often do you beat yourself up, put yourself down, and limit your potential? Can you accurately state how many times you are consciously and unconsciously pessimistic about yourself? When your unconscious negativity drives your actions, you are blind to its destruction on yourself and your surroundings.

To shift your energy using this energetic principle, you must first become conscious of your communication patterns, internally and externally. Enroll others around you to do the same, so you can all hold each other accountable when you externally project. For the internal journey, challenge yourself and get creative. Maybe it's time to revisit your childhood swear jar, but this time it's about the destructive energy coming from your thoughts. By bringing your judgments to the forefront of your attention, you can then lead with love and rephrase. Keysha's journey outlined how leading with love can convert negative apathy to positive results.

How else can leading with love shift your energy? In Chapter 8, I outlined how leaders can align opposing team members to ensure they work towards the same vision and goals. In addition to cultivating curiosity, the energetic principle of leading with love can also bridge gaps of opposing sides. How so? While it's easy to focus on your differences when you're opposite "your enemy," leading with love allows you to use a different lens, to focus on your similarities. When you align on various values and life events, even if you don't agree, an energetic shift will occur, creating a shared understanding and respect.

The five energetic principles are here to instruct you on how to effectively shift your energy to address short-term and sustainable challenges. By leveraging them, you will discover the power of your influence on yourself, just by exercising control over your thoughts, emotions, and actions. Use these lessons learned as a "how to" reference guide to continue to work on shifting your energy to serve you versus deplete you.

Action Steps and Takeaways

1. What are the five energetic success principles shared throughout this chapter?
   - The Principle of Detachment
   - Practice Presence
   - Create Possibility
   - Cultivate Curiosity
   - Lead with Love (or Care)

2. How can you use the principle of detachment to detach from a limiting belief?

3. What is one way you want to practice being present in the upcoming month?

4. How can you cultivate curiosity to better understand a challenge and create a solution?

5. What is one thing that you don't believe is possible, that you truly would love in your life? How can you bring that possibility to life?

Final Thoughts

The first step in shifting one's personal energy is understanding your current energetic state. Once you identify your initial conscious or unconscious thoughts and emotions, you gain the power to choose your actions and decide what level of energy you want to experience and exercise. This is the power of these energetic success principles. They empower your choice when you don't feel in control.

Each example above demonstrated how an individual's perception of a situation ignited their initial reaction. Some experienced defeat, some were ready to put their gloves up, some threw in the towel and settled with complacency, and some led with inquiry seeking to learn and grow. Post initial reaction is where each and every one gained control. This too, will happen to you. With practice, shifting becomes easier, quicker, and sometimes, even replaces your original reaction.

12

How to Build a Motivational Workplace Culture

I'm tellin' everybody
I'm 'bout to explode, take off this load
Spin it, bust it open, won't ya make it go
And I just quit my job
Damn, they work me so damn hard
Work by nine, then off past five
And they work my nerves
That's why I cannot sleep at night
You won't break my soul.[1]

In 2022, Beyoncé released "Break My Soul," embodying the voices of millions of workers worldwide. The "State of the Global Workplace: 2023 Report" calculated the estimated loss in profits from poor leadership and disengaged employees equated to "9% loss of our global GDP—enough to make a difference between success and a failure for humanity."[2] When asked what organizations can do to literally change the world, Gallup had one answer: "Change the way your people are managed."[2]

Here is the change the workforce needs. It's time for an energetic shift. Throughout this book, you have discovered the definition of personal energy—constructive and destructive. We walked through all seven zones of energy, with descriptions, examples, and key takeaways to ensure you can identify how you are experiencing a situation from your thoughts, emotions, and actions. From there, I demonstrated how to use five energetic success principles to empower you to choose your personal energy, so you are in control, versus your energy controlling you.

Now it's time to take these lessons to your workforce so individuals, teams, and leaders can build, grow, and enhance constructive energy in your workplace. Here's how to build and sustain a motivational workplace culture to execute on your organization's vision, mission, and goals with energy and passion. As Beyoncé sang:

> I'm lookin' for motivation
> I'm lookin' for a new foundation, yeah
> And I'm on that new vibration
> I'm buildin' my own foundation, yeah.

Conduct a Workplace Investigation

Every day, the media publishes articles hypothesizing the future of the workplace. They bring in expert after expert, providing predictions and statistics. So why is this question still so unanswered? The future of the workplace isn't going to be one way or another. The traditional brick-and-mortar office job has been transforming for years, and thanks to the transformations that resulted from the pandemic, the workplace as we knew it will never be the same.

Thank goodness! As we saw with the Great Resignation, we needed a huge upgrade to our workplace software and hardware. There has been a growing misalignment of values between companies and their people. Both organizations and people want to succeed and feel accomplished by the work they provide and do. Yet the energy behind the "how" is not aligning.

How do we address this gap? The first step is to recognize the role personal energy plays in the workplace. In Chapter 1, personal energy was defined as the amount of vigor or capacity an individual brings to a situation. It is based on the way someone perceives certain situations, which, in turn, is forged by their life history, training, and genetic makeup.

Destructive energy often arises in frustration, self-doubt, and burnout. When experiencing low levels of energy, many resort to flight, fight, or freeze responses. This stressful energy state often results in an inability to see the potential for a positive outcome and can generate a scarcity versus abundance mindset. Constructive personal energy fuels growth, inspiring a productive workplace culture and environment.

Shifting to constructive energy can empower individuals to improve their focus and accomplish their goals. By learning how your workforce's inherent perspectives and biases shape reactions within your culture, you can enable people to choose differently, in ways that increase motivation and drive the actions needed for success. Organizations can support shifts in personal energy through internal and external means and at three different levels: executive, manager, and individual. Conducting an Energy Leadership Assessment throughout your workforce generates a hot spot analysis. From there, focused resources can be allocated to support each hot spot's needs to shift their energy from negative to positive.

How can your organization ensure that destructive energy isn't stemming from your company's foundation? Conduct an audit of your company's policies, procedures, and practices. Do they prioritize the following values?

- Inclusion
- Flexibility
- Efficiency
- Transparency
- Honesty

These are the top five values of your evolving workforce. As you identify opportunities, infuse these into your workforce's core to fuel your employee's personal energy, cultivating a motivational workplace culture.

Inclusion

Inclusion in the workplace fosters an environment where people from all different intersectional identities feel welcome, valued, and integrated into a company's culture. Inclusive environments ensure that every person has equitable access, not only to opportunities, but to contributions. Inclusive organizations promote diversity of thought and communication styles, stemming from each person's life journey. The differences are not only recognized but celebrated!

When you cultivate an inclusive workplace culture, people appreciate each other's unique contributions to advancing psychological safety and a sense of belonging within your workplace community. Experts Janet B. Reid, PhD, and Vincent R. Brown define inclusion as "leveraging the power of a group's diversity to attain a common goal or objective. It is not about people blending in—corporate 'fit' and assimilation are yesterday's thinking."[3]

Through their Intrinsic Inclusion Certification, Brown and Reid outline four bias disruptors to reboot an individual's brain to become naturally motivated towards those who aren't like them. What did we learn in Chapter 3? Our thoughts and emotions lead to action. When we take the time to lead with curiosity to shift our inherently biased perspectives, we can shift our actions, and therefore not only our own energy but also the energy around us.

How can energizing inclusion enhance your organization's energy?

Inclusive workplaces welcome people from diverse backgrounds, including different races, ethnicities, genders, sexual orientations, abilities, ages, and socioeconomic statuses. Christina Donelson, CHRO at Moore, emphasizes how inclusion is essential to energizing the workforce. She highlights that inclusion "paves the path to a culture of belonging, where every individual's unique contribution is nurtured and valued. Belonging is a fundamental human need, woven into the fabric of our beings. It's in spaces where we can freely embrace our true selves that we discover genuine fulfillment and purpose. When individuals feel a deep sense of belonging, their authenticity radiates, igniting a vibrant tapestry of creativity, fueling boundless passion, and propelling us toward meaningful change."[4] This vibrant tapestry of creativity that Christina references is a catalyst for collaborative ideation, distinctive insights, and innovative solutions.

How do collaborative ideation, distinctive insights, and innovative solutions positively impact an organization? When individuals and teams know they can advance their company's vision and goals, they become motivated and engaged to operate at higher levels of energy, resulting in increased productivity and performance. When employees feel empowered and driven to execute a company's vision and goals, employees, stakeholders, board members, and customers can explicitly see how a company walks their talk, fueling their mission, a social responsibility to the betterment of society.

Flexibility

If we had to pick one takeaway from Covid-19 in the workplace, I believe we would all agree that flexibility skyrocketed to the top of the importance chart, both for employees and employers. Pre-pandemic, SHRM reported around 2% of the workforce was remote. Around 30% of the workforce is remote as of 2023, with hybrid models becoming more popular based on each industry's operational needs.[5]

Flexibility in the workplace provides employees with the ability to have choices. Depending on the role, this can include independence in managing their schedules and methods of work, as well as work environment and location. As the workplace continues to recruit future generations, we will continue to see more flexible options emerge, mirroring the flexible options currently offered within our educational institutions. How does flexibility energize a workforce?

Flexibility promotes work-life balance, ensuring your employees can expend their energy in alignment with their values. Rather than having to choose between personal and professional goals, employees can now take ownership of their time-management skills and accomplish both. When a person can focus on one assignment, whether that is completing a project or spending quality time with their family, they can dedicate 100% of their energy to that task, fully present. The energetic impact of allowing people to be present in both their personal and professional lives leads to lower stress levels in the workplace, which increases your organization's energy, job satisfaction, and overall well-being.

When employees have more autonomy over their work schedule, they can also optimize their energy to be most productive.

Formerly, the workplace modeled a one-size-fits-all schedule for each role, versus a personal schedule. One-size-fits-all doesn't work in retail and doesn't work in our workplace. The personalization flexibility provided to each person ensures they can work the hours when they are most energized, as well as in locations that are most energizing. This includes taking energetic breaks, which, as we saw in Chapter 7, is essential to keeping your battery running and avoiding burnout.

Flexibility in the workplace is a huge differentiator, becoming a driver to attracting and retaining talent. Rather than having to rely on talent within miles of a business office location, companies can now recruit people from all over ths US, or even the rest of the world, based on the role. Flexibility promotes DEIA, as it accommodates diverse lifestyles and needs. In terms of accessibility, flexibility is transformational for someone who qualifies for ADA, both physically and mentally, or is a caregiver for someone under ADA.

Flexibility within recruitment can also save a company money. Nick Depner, director of sales for United Airlines, emphasized this advantage as he continues to grow his team. "If your top candidate is in Des Moines, Iowa, and wants to stay there, why should that be an issue if the role is remote? It costs the company a lot more money to pay market prices in NYC compared to many other cities."[6] Not to mention that your candidate is happy, because they can perform their job where they're most energized.

For employers, flexibility brings several advantages. If your organization is 100% remote, or hybrid, your commercial real estate (CRE) costs decrease substantially. If you are a start-up or small business, flexibility can also be essential for your business model. By eliminating the pressure of having to forecast space needs for a growing or shrinking company, you can focus your energy on growing the people you have supporting your business.

Flexibility also reduces absenteeism, allowing individuals to rearrange their schedule for health concerns, or unforeseen events, rather than having to take the entire day off. Reduced absenteeism ensures that teams can continue to operate as designed, with less disruptions to an operation's workflow. Most importantly, flexibility directly correlates to a decrease in turnover. With your people being your most expensive cost, a decrease of even 2% can save an organization hundreds of thousands to millions of dollars annually.

"Flexibility creates opportunity. Opportunity to find the best talent. Opportunity to save money. Opportunity to be innovative," exclaims Depner. Ultimately, flexibility benefits both the employee and the employer. Because of flexibility, both are better positioned to adjust to the ever-changing needs of their customers, employees, and business.

Efficiency

Technology advances have made efficiency in our personal lives non-negotiable. However, the workplace has responded quite a bit more slowly to this requirement. As future generations continue to permeate the workforce, leveraging artificial intelligence (AI) to automate processes will become a required sustainable business practice. Why? To start, future generations won't have to "be patient" and adjust to the learning curve of transitioning from paper to electronic processes the way Boomers, Gen X, and even Millennials have had to do.

We see this now with job applications and the "easy apply" button. Why would someone spend hours manually inputting their resume when features exist to autofill this information into a company's applicant tracking system (ATS). This one efficiency reduces the time it takes to backfill a role substantially. Efficient business practices like this directly correlate to an organization's bottom line. Not only with their employees, but also with their customers. How do efficient business practices energize the workplace?

Efficiency enhances productivity. When workflows and processes are streamlined, employees can operate in flow and optimize their energy. How so? Efficient processes enable employees with time management skills, so they can forecast deliverables with their energy and output. Ensuring proactive practices are in place reduces the amount of unplanned occurrences that can take place, decreasing employee and team stress levels, which decreases the destructive energy in your workplace.

As we all know, frustration from inefficient processes heightens individuals' destructive energy. When an employee can focus on their role versus navigating a broken ecosystem, their energy goes towards the task at hand. The energy and time that is wasted from disorganization increases employee stress levels, directly enhancing poor communication in the workplace. In "The Cost of Poor Communication," David Grossman estimated a loss of $62.4 million per year in companies with 100,000 employees. Poor communication costs companies fewer than 100 employees an average of $420,000 per year.[7]

Customers and employees correlate efficiency with quality. When business practices are simplified, standardized, monitored, and audited, there's less room for inaccuracies and deficiencies. Quality products and services lead to customer satisfaction. Why is the Amazon buying experience so sought after, both with customers and employees? Efficient processes plus verified quality feedback equals customer satisfaction plus continuous improvement.

By energizing continuous improvement through employee and customer feedback loops, organizations can adapt quickly to evolving market demands. Over time, we have seen how the use of data analytics and artificial intelligence provides companies with the ability to forecast future trends. When innovative solutions can be designed in anticipation of these trends, companies hold a competitive advantage. We have seen this consistently with Apple, each time they release a product to market.

Ultimately, efficient companies can ensure the right number of people are in the right number of jobs. "Labor costs can account for as much as 70% of total business costs; this includes employee wages, benefits, payroll and other related taxes."[8] With efficient business practices in place, companies can maximize the utilization of their resources, resulting in higher profits and long-term financial success. Kaitlyn Jones, in-house counsel and head of HR for Fletcher Jones Automotive, outlines how she empowered HR to lead the charge with efficient business practices, transforming the culture of her organization. "The reason I found it so important to implement systems like Compli and PayScale and hire leadership roles to standardize company policies and practices, was to ensure our people could focus on their jobs. In turn, this changed our company's understanding of human resources. Understanding our people's needs and creating efficiencies to address those needs drives our strategy, engagement, productivity, and revenue."[9]

In summary, efficiency in the workplace plays a pivotal role in enhancing productivity, reducing costs, optimizing resources, improving quality, boosting employee morale, and fostering innovation. Organizations that prioritize and cultivate efficiency gain a competitive advantage in today's fast-paced and dynamic business environment.

Transparency

Why is transparency a new driving value in the workplace? For the first time ever, we have a generation that was born with the internet. Access to soliciting and providing information has never been easier. If your organization is hiding something, Gen Z will find it. Secondly, "concerns over fake news or false information being used as a weapon is now at an all-time high."[10] Transparency combats #fakenews and instills trust.

Tracy West, VP and general manager, Product Madness Americas Studio, links transparency directly to energy. "When company leadership isn't transparent with their team members, the team can feel that energy and trust begin to erode."[11] During her time as VP of Enterprise HR at Pinnacle Entertainment (PNK), she led the people transition throughout the $2.8 billion merger and acquisition (M&A), reporting directly to Anthony Sanfilippo, CEO of Pinnacle Entertainment. In reflecting on her time throughout the M&A, she shared that often, there are very valid reasons for leadership not to be fully transparent, especially in publicly traded companies, where confidentiality is incredibly important. "For companies to thrive in this new way of working, this is when leadership needs to step up and not back, no matter how hard it is. They need to open lines of communication and be present even if they can't be fully transparent. So, when the information that could not be shared does come out, it is coming from a present leader, which makes it much easier to comprehend and accept."

When your employees know your organization is transparent, they can focus their energy executing on your company's values, mission, and goals. When individuals are fearful of inequities and hidden practices, their energy becomes divided, pulling from their focus to advance company initiatives. Laws are even changing to ensure your workforce policies and practices are transparent.

As of 2023, a variety of states including Washington, California, Nevada, Maryland, Connecticut, Rhode Island, and New York have enacted legislation that employers must include the pay range for each role they post in the job description. Numerous other states have also mandated that employers must disclose salaries if an employee requests compensation information. In my TEDx talk "Building a Motivational Workplace Culture: Reinventing Compensation,"[12] through personal stories and data, I showcase how a company can increase their employees' energy, productivity, and retention, when both employees and employers embrace the value of transparency.

On a scale of 1 to 10 (1 being the lowest and 10 being the highest), how transparent are the rest of your company's policies and procedures? In addition to pay transparency, it is imperative that organizations build transparent practices into their performance management and evaluation process. How can companies ensure their performance management and evaluation processes are transparent?

One of the most important lessons I learned from my leadership at PNK was that no one should ever be surprised if they are getting separated from the company. If they were, we knew something wasn't transparent and took immediate action to investigate where we failed as an employer. Look at your performance management forms. Does your coaching or disciplinary process clearly outline requirements, advancements, and consequences between verbal and written documentation? If your company has embraced a coaching philosophy, are requirements clearly defined to ensure you manage up versus manage out your employees? When this process is truly transparent, coaching addresses both an employee's and a leader's concerns, opportunities, milestones, and next steps.

The same goes for promotions and bonus allocations. Whether you do the nine-box exercise, scorecards, or personal development plans to leverage your teams' goals and achievements to bonus out or promote an employee, it's important that every team member understand their objectives. These targets should be continuously discussed, and a team member should have no doubt about how they're performing against agreed upon landmarks. This level of transparency requires honesty and finesse with crucial conversations, which leads me to our next non-negotiable value: honesty.

Honesty

Prioritize honesty over harmony. This change will be the hardest, and the most impactful. Similar to how our media has shifted from truth to public relations (PR), our workplaces have created its own PR spin on its definition of honesty. In doing so, conversations lack depth, masking the destructive energy under the apparent harmony. If someone were to light a match under harmony, an explosion of truth like a cannon of confetti would occur all around us.

How am I defining honesty in the workplace? Honesty starts with always telling the truth. The truth to your employees, leaders, shareholders, board members, customers, and yourself. Dishonesty includes stealing, cheating, and omitting information. It takes courage and ownership to be authentic, before, during, even after a challenge arises.

Why is this going to be the most difficult? Businesses are being held to the higher standards, as they are seen as the most trusted amongst institutions. Because of this trust, individuals are now demanding that companies should "leverage their competitive advantage to inform debate and deliver solutions across climate, diversity and inclusion, and skill training."[13] We see this in company corporate sustainability reports, which are becoming even more strict, since the new direction announced on January 5, 2023, in the Corporate Sustainability Report Directive (CSRD).

In addition to Corporate Sustainability Reports, employees are asking for companies to host events such as town halls and lunch-and-learns to foster communication and understanding of breaking news. Why is this so challenging? It comes down to opening the floor to courageous conversations, which most are not comfortable with. What did we learn about the Safety Zone? Avoiding crucial conversations does not make problems go away. In fact, all you're doing is wasting energy. What did we learn about the Compromise Zone? You can put glitter over garbage all you want. The garbage is still there and needs to be addressed before anyone can move forward. "When you think of fierce conversations, think passion, integrity, authenticity, collaboration. Think cultural transformation."[14]

What are some tools you can use to start ensuring your organization can foster courageous conversations? To start, it's important that employees understand the difference between a debate, a discussion, and a dialogue. This way, they understand which tools to leverage to find a shared connection, to enhance their working relationship. When you're in a dialogue, you aren't trying to prove someone else wrong. You are working towards a shared goal to progress your company's vision and mission.

Use tools such as the LARA[15] Method (Listen, Affirm, Respond, Add) to host trainings so various perspectives can practice communicating their differences and understandings of assorted challenges. Leverage technology to institute a two-way feedback system that is transparent and promotes collaboration towards a shared goal. Hire mental health professionals—whether they're specialists in psychology, therapy, and/or coaching—to enhance your organization's communication well-being.

Invest in building a sustainable ecosystem of constructive energetic communication to ensure your company is set up for long-term success. This is how we can create an energetic shift in our workplace, and work with each other versus against each other, towards shared goals. Honesty over harmony will elevate your workplace culture to building sustainable business practices and a motivational workplace culture. As Beyoncé tells us:

> Release ya anger, release ya mind
> Release ya job, release the time
> Release ya trade, release the stress
> Release the love, forget the rest

Workplace motivation and productivity are a direct result of employees discovering how their personal energy level impacts themselves and their teams, helping them gauge, control, and modify their reactions. As shown in Figure 12.1, individuals with high constructive energy are statistically more satisfied with their lives across 14 success indicators, which directly impacts a company's bottom line. Shifting from a destructive (catabolic) to a constructive (anabolic) profile (as an individual) can increase

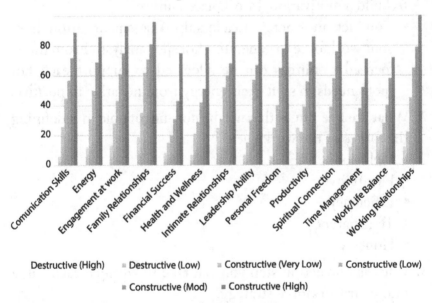

FIGURE 12.1   Work and Life Satisfaction Across 14 Success Indicators

Source: Adapted from Replication Study: Key Factor Revealed for Determining Success in Work and in Life." IPEC. https://www.ipeccoaching.com/hubfs/iPEC-Key-Factor-Study-June-2013.pdf

engagement at work by as much as 51%.[16] It can also improve satisfaction with work-life balance and working relationships (by 70% and 44%, respectively).

Organizations vary in how they are tapping into the benefits of personal energy. I created the Energetic Impact Index[17] as a way to illustrate and define organization's energy leadership maturity to help them advance from basic to leading edge. As organizations become more advanced at improving and leveraging employees' personal energy to drive action and fulfill goals at work, employee engagement, retention, productivity, and overall business results will improve.

Action Steps and Takeaways

1. What is the first step your team and/or company should take to build a motivational workplace culture?
   - Conduct an Energy Leadership Assessment throughout your workforce to generate a hot spot analysis. From there, focused resources can be allocated to support each hot spot's needs to shift their energy from negative to positive.

2. What are five values that will be non-negotiable in redefining the future of the workplace?
   - Inclusion
   - Flexibility
   - Efficiency
   - Transparency
   - Honesty

3. What is one action step you can take to advance each value into your workforce strategy?

- Inclusion:

  _____

- Flexibility:

  _____

- Efficiency:

  _____

- Transparency:

  _____

- Honesty:

  _____

Final Thoughts

Here is the change the workforce needs! Constructive personal energy is the answer to shifting the "State of the Global Workplace" report. Now that you have discovered the seven zones of energy and the associated energetic principles to create shifts in your own energy, it's time to take these lessons to your workforce so individuals, teams, and leaders can build, grow, and enhance constructive energy in your workplace. In the words of Martin Luther, we all know "how soon 'not now' becomes 'never'!"[18] We can't afford to wait. The success of our humanity depends on it. You have the tools. You have the resources. You have the energy! Cannonball into action and build a sustainable motivational workplace culture to execute on your own and your organizations vision, mission, and goals with energy and passion. We turn once more to Beyoncé:

> Got motivation
> I done found me a new foundation, yeah
> I'm takin' my new salvation
> And I'm build my own foundation, yeah.

Notes

Chapter 1

1. Buffet, J. (2002). "What If the Hokey Pokey Is All It Really Is About?" *Far Side of the World*. All other lyrics quoted in this chapter are from this song.
2. Gallup, Inc. (2023). "State of the Global Workplace Report." https://www.gallup.com/workplace/349484/state-of-the-global-workplace.aspx?thank-you-report-form=1

Chapter 2

1. Gallup, Inc. (2023). "State of the Global Workplace Report." https://www.gallup.com/workplace/349484/state-of-the-global-workplace.aspx?thank-you-report-form=1
2. Worqdrive. (2022). "WORQDRIVE Reveals the True Cost of Employee Turnover in Dynamic Job Market." GlobeNewswire News Room. https://www.globenewswire.com/en/news-release/2022/07/19/2481615/0/en/WORQDRIVE-Reveals-the-True-Cost-of-Employee-Turnover-in-Dynamic-Job-Market.html

Chapter 3

1. Kelly, J. (2019). "People Don't Leave Bad Jobs, They Leave Bad Bosses: Here's How To Be A Better Manager To Maintain And Motivate Your Team." *Forbes*. https://www.forbes.com/sites/jackkelly/2019/11/22/people-dont-leave-bad-jobs-they-leave-bad-bosses-heres-how-to-be-a-better-manager-to-maintain-and-motivate-your-team/?sh=46f067ec22b9

2. "Values-Driven Solution Assessment." (n.d.). https://www.dropbox.com/s/28rz13jj5dt9s0p/Values%20Driven%20Solution%20Assessment%20Final.pdf?dl=0

3. Brown, B. (2015). *Rising Strong: The Reckoning. The Rumble. The Revolution.* Vermilion.

Chapter 4

1. "Remarks by the First Lady at an Event with Elizabeth Garrett Anderson Students." (2011, May 25). Stylist.co.uk. https://www.stylist.co.uk/long-reads/michelle-obama-impostor-syndrome-career-advice-work-mental-health-relationships-becoming-book-us/240417/

2. Television Academy. (2022, September 13). 74th Emmy Awards [Video]. https://www.youtube.com/watch?v=zdWc-MW4HCM

3. Morin, A. (Ed.). (2017, October 12). "Why It's Hard to Let Go of Your Self-Limiting Beliefs." *Psychology Today*. https://www.psychologytoday.com/intl/blog/what-mentally-strong-people-dont-do/201710/why-its-hard-let-go-your-self-limiting-beliefs

4. World Health Organization: WHO. (2019, May 28). "Burn-out an 'occupational phenomenon': International Classification of Diseases." https://www.who.int/news/item/28-05-2019-burn-out-an-occupational-phenomenon-international-classification-of-diseases

5. "Anatomy of Work Special Report: The unexplored link between imposter syndrome and burnout." (2022). https://resources.asana.com/americas-anatomy-of-work-burnout-ebook.html

6. Brower, T., PhD. (2022, July 24). "Burnout Is A Worldwide Problem: 5 Ways Work Must Change." *Forbes*. https://www.forbes.com/sites/tracybrower/2022/07/24/burnout-is-a-worldwide-problem-5-ways-work-must-change/?sh=15b4d29c6c1e

7. "Values-Driven Solution Assessment." (n.d.). https://www.dropbox.com/s/28rz13jj5dt9s0p/Values%20Driven%20Solution%20Assessment%20Final.pdf?dl=0

Chapter 5

1. Scott, K. (2017). *Radical Candor: Be a Kick-Ass Boss Without Losing Your Humanity*. St Martin's Press.

2. "Just Cause." Practical Law. (n.d.). https://content.next.westlaw.com/practical-law/document/I073b9c5288e811ec9f24ec7b211d8087/Just-Cause?viewType=FullText&transitionType=Default&contextData=(sc.Default)&firstPage=true

3. UN News. (2022, June 17). "Nearly one billion people have a mental disorder: WHO." https://news.un.org/en/story/2022/06/1120682

4. Wilson, T. D. (2004). *Strangers to Ourselves: Discovering the Adaptive Unconscious*. Belknap Press. https://doi.org/10.4159/9780674045217

5. Career Diversity. (2022, April 14). T-Mobile. https://careers.t-mobile.com/culture-and-benefits/diversity-2/

6. Textio. (n/d). "Hire and retain a diverse team." https://textio.com/

7. Textio.com. (n/d). Case studies. https://textio.com/resources/case-studies?dialog=t-mobile-scales-dei-impact

8. Giacomazzo, B. (2022, May 30). "The Fortune 500 List Has A 'Record Number' Of Black CEOs—But There's Still Only 6 Of Them." AfroTech. https://afrotech.com/fortune-500-black-ceos

9. Center for WorkLife Law at UC Hastings College of the Law. (n.d.). "Gender Bias Learning Project: Maternal Wall." https://genderbiasbingo.com/maternal-wall/#.Y8ch23bMI2w

10. Stewart, A. (2023). "2023 Gender Pay Gap Report." https://www.payscale.com/research-and-insights/gender-pay-gap/

11. Hirsch, W. (2020). "Five questions about psychological safety, answered." ScienceForWork. https://scienceforwork.com/blog/psychological-safety/

12. Coyle, D. (2019). *The Culture Code: The Secrets of Highly Successful Groups*. Random House.

13. Dobrilova, T. (2023, July 3). "15 Disturbing Workplace Violence Statistics for 2023." Techjury. https://techjury.net/blog/workplace-violence-statistics/#gref

Chapter 6

1. Greve, P. (2019, October 24). "Careers of the Future: The jobs that don't exist yet." Forward Edge. https://www.forward-edge.net/careers-of-the-future-the-jobs-that-dont-exist-yet/

Chapter 7

1. Hyken, S. *Become Your Own Superhero* podcast (2022, July 1). "The one statistic that matters most is if the customer comes back!" https://podcasts.apple.com/au/podcast/the-one-statistic-that-matters-most-is-if-the/id1511122216?i=1000579614906

2. "Wheel of Life." (n.d.). https://www.dropbox.com/s/kali42kp9ujahjj/Wheel%20of%20Life.pdf?dl=0

3. "Values-Driven Solution Assessment." (n.d.). https://www.dropbox.com/s/28rz13jj5dt9s0p/Values%20Driven%20Solution%20Assessment%20Final.pdf?dl=0

Chapter 8

1. TEDx Talks. (2022, January 7). "Building a Motivational Workplace Culture: Reinventing Compensation." https://www.youtube.com/watch?v=lakwCL5zSm4
2. Carrie Matthews, personal communication, July 18, 2023.
3. "2023 Global Human Capital Trends." (2023). Deloitte Malta. https://www2.deloitte.com/mt/en/pages/human-capital/articles/introduction-human-capital-trends.html

Chapter 9

1. National Geographic. (2021, April 13). "Bonus Episode: The secret culture of killer whales." https://www.nationalgeographic.com/podcasts/article/bonus-episode-the-secret-culture-of-killer-whales
2. Allegiant Travel 2014 Annual Report. (2015). https://ir.allegiantair.com/static-files/cdc7fd5f-d7fb-4530-850a-19b682f80d37
3. Alex Cheney, personal communication, April 19, 2023.
4. Mark Grock, personal communication, July 11, 2023.
5. Mihaly Csikszentmihalyi quote: "'Flow' is the way people describe their state of mind when consciousness is harmoniously ordered, and they want to pursue whatever they are doing for its own sake." https://quotefancy.com/quote/2194140/Mihaly-Csikszentmihalyi-Flow-is-the-way-people-describe-their-state-of-mind-when
6. Freehling, E. (2022, August 10). To Win the Talent Race, It's Time to Get to Know Gen Z. Darden Report Online. https://news.darden.virginia.edu/2022/08/10/its-time-to-get-to-know-gen-z/
7. Monash Business School. (2023, April 3). Marketing dictionary: "Phygital." https://www.monash.edu/business/marketing/marketing-dictionary/p/phygital
8. Selina. (n.d.). "What Is Selina?" https://whatis.selina.com/
9. Schroeder, B. (2021, December 28). "The Fitness Industry Has Been Here Forever. What's Changed And How Entrepreneurs And Small Business Owners Can Leverage New Trends." *Forbes*. https://www.forbes.com/sites/bernhardschroeder/2021/12/28/the-fitness-industry-has-been-here-forever-whats-changed-and-how-entrepreneurs-and-small-business-owners-can-leverage-new-trends/?sh=276712c745a7
10. SoulCycle. "Soul Etiquette: Respect. Joy. Love." https://www.soul-cycle.com/soulconnected/etiquette/
11. Csikszentmihalyi, M. *Flow: The Psychology of Optimal Experience*. Harper Perennial, 2008.

Chapter 10

1. Ramiz Ahmed, personal communication, June 14, 2023.
2. Mindful Communications. (2023, January 6). "Getting Started with Mindfulness." https://www.mindful.org/meditation/mindfulness-getting-started/#:~:text=Mindfulness%20is%20the%20basic%20human,what's%20going%20on%20around%20us
3. Global Wellness Institute. (2023, August 21). "What Is Wellness?" https://globalwellnessinstitute.org/what-is-wellness/
4. *APA Dictionary of Psychology*. (n.d.). https://dictionary.apa.org/meditation
5. Chad Goffstein, personal communication, July 11, 2023.
6. Novotney, A. (2023, April 21). "Why mental health needs to be a top priority in the workplace." https://www.apa.org/news/apa/2022/surgeon-general-workplace-well-being
7. Karey Larsen, personal communication, July 11, 2023.
8. Sinek, S., Mead, D., and Docker, P. (2017). *Find Your Why: A Practical Guide for Discovering Purpose for You and Your Team*. Portfolio.
9. Welch, J., and Byrne, J. (2001b). *Jack: Straight from the Gut*. chrome-extension://efaidnbmnnnibpcajpcglclefindmkaj/http://dspace.vnbrims.org:13000/jspui/bitstream/123456789/4730/1/Jack%20Straight%20from%20the%20Gut.pdf
10. National Geographic. (2021, April 13). "Bonus Episode: The secret culture of killer whales." https://www.nationalgeographic.com/podcasts/article/bonus-episode-the-secret-culture-of-killer-whales
11. Brian Skerry, personal communication, April 18, 2023.

Chapter 11

1. Tony, T. (2022, September 8). "Where Focus Goes, Energy Flows." https://www.tonyrobbins.com/career-business/where-focus-goes-energy-flows/#:~:text=As%20Tony%20Robbins%20says%2C%20energy,your%20energy%2C%20amazing%20things%20happen
2. Barry Thomas, personal communication, June 27, 2023.
3. Healthcare Financial Management Association. (2023, July 27). Metropolitan New York Chapter. https://www.hfma.org/chapters/region-2/metropolitan-new-york/
4. The Cosmopolitan. (n.d.). Top 11 Reasons to Work at the Cosmopolitan." https://www.cosmopolitanlasvegas.com/careers/top-reasons
5. Finnegan, A. (2010, October 22). "Cosmopolitan's jarring ad aimed at the 'curious class.'" *Las Vegas Sun*. https://lasvegassun.com/news/2010/oct/22/cosmopolitans-strange-ad-aimed-curious-class/

Chapter 12

1. "Break My Soul." Lyrics and Music by Beyoncé arranged by gjcov. (n.d.). https://www.smule.com/song/beyonce-break-my-soul-karaoke-lyrics/17331047_17331047/arrangement
2. Gallup, Inc. (2023b). "State of the Global Workplace: 2023 Report." https://www.gallup.com/workplace/349484/state-of-the-global-workplace.aspx
3. Reid, Janet B., and Brown, Vincent R. (2021). *Intrinsic Inclusion: Rebooting Your Biased Bain.* New Phoenix Publishing.
4. Christina Donelson, personal communication, July 17, 2023.
5. "SHRM: The Voice of All Things Work." (2023, June 21). https://www.shrm.org/pages/default.aspx
6. Nick Depner, personal communication, July 13, 2023.
7. SHRM. (2020). "The Cost of Poor Communications." https://www.shrm.org/resourcesandtools/hr-topics/behavioral-competencies/communication/pages/the-cost-of-poor-communications.aspx
8. Paycor. (n.d.). "The Biggest Cost of Doing Business: A Closer Look at Labor Costs." https://www.paycor.com/resource-center/articles/closer-look-at-labor-costs/
9. Kaitlyn Jones, personal communication, July 13, 2023.
10. "2022 Edelman Trust Barometer." (2022, January 24). https://www.edelman.com/trust/2022-trust-barometer
11. Tracy West, personal communication, July 12, 2023.
12. Ahmed, R. (n.d.). "Building a Motivational Workplace Culture: Reinventing Compensation." TED Talk. https://www.ted.com/talks/rebecca_ahmed_building_a_motivational_workplace_culture_reinventing_compensation
13. "2023 Edelman Trust Barometer." (2023). chrome-extension://efaidnbmnnnibpcajpcglclefindmkaj/https://www.edelman.com/sites/g/files/aatuss191/files/2023-03/2023%20Edelman%20Trust%20Barometer%20Global%20Report%20FINAL.pdf
14. Scott, S. (2002). *Fierce Conversations: Achieving Success at Work and in Life One Conversation at a Time.* Berkley.
15. "The LARA Method for Managing Tense Talks." Stanford SPARQtools. https://sparqtools.org/lara/
16. "New Study by iPEC Coaching Reveals Key Indicator for Greatest Satisfaction." (2011, May 10). PRWeb. https://www.prweb.com/releases/2011/5/prweb8405548.htm
17. "Are you struggling to keep your employees engaged and productive?" https://www.energeticimpact.com/consulting-3/
18. Martin Luther. (n.d.). https://www.goodreads.com/quotes/452090-how-soon-not-now-becomes-never#:~:text=Quote%20by%20Martin%20Luther%3A%20%E2%80%9CHow,now'%20becomes%20'never'!%E2%80%9D

About the Author

Rebecca Ahmed is an award-winning speaker, a business consultant, and an Energy Leadership Index™ Master Practitioner (ELI-MP), which is an exclusive training in human energy and how we can experience, express, and expand it in ourselves and others. Rebecca is also a Professional Certified Coach (PCC) with the International Coaching Federation (ICF).

Her deep real-world expertise derives from a decade plus spent as an HR (People Services) leader at some of the largest hospitality and travel organizations worldwide, including the Cosmopolitan of Las Vegas, a Marriott Autograph Collection, Pinnacle Entertainment, and Allegiant Airlines.

During her tenure as a People Services leader in Hospitality, Rebecca is most notable for helping to guide executives through the $2.8 billion merger and acquisition (M&A) to Boyd Gaming Corporation and Penn National Gaming. At Pinnacle Entertainment, she led the team's HR Operations and HR Technology integration for approximately 16,000-plus team members.

Today, Rebecca advises companies of all sizes on how to create a motivational workplace culture by transforming the energy and enthusiasm of their teams. She excels at helping companies to:

- Rediscover and accomplish their work with passion and an innate sense of joy.

- Craft a positive culture by inspiring employees to positively influence and uplift those around them.

- Exercise their freedom to express themselves without being self-conscious.

- Shift their focus from dwelling on challenges to innovating and communicating solutions.

- Help employees understand how to control their responses to external factors that tempt them off track emotionally.

- Facilitate a greater flow of positive energy levels at home and at work, so that each employee has the best chance to excel at their job.

Under her direct supervision, Allegiant Airlines won Glassdoor's "Best Places to Interview" award. In acceptance of this award, Rebecca was featured as a panelist on "Hire Better Talent Faster: How to Optimize Your Employer Brand and Candidate Apply Process."

Caesars Entertainment, the largest casino-entertainment company in the US retained Rebecca as their new "Chief Energy Officer" in 2021. Her role included speaking twice monthly on how to shift their emerging leaders' energies from surviving to thriving using energetic principles at their Emerging Leader Summits across their 55 US-based properties.

Rebecca is proud to share her "fight on cheer" from the University of Southern California (USC) and master's degree from the University of Nevada, Las Vegas (UNLV). Rebecca's passion for philanthropy awarded her Top Volunteer at the Cosmopolitan of Las Vegas from 2011 to 2013, and she served as an advisory board member of the HR Exchange Network from 2016 to 2018.

Rebecca was born and raised in Las Vegas. She is the oldest of nine children and thus began her people management career quite early in life.

Values-Driven Solution Assessment

This assessment can also be accessed at https://www.energe ticimpact.com/values-driven-solution-assessment/.

What Are Values?

Values are your personal motivators. They are the principles or standards that you hold to the utmost importance. They drive you towards your goals, purpose, and mission.

Why Is It Important to Identify and Define My Values?

Discovering and defining your personal values in your own words will give you the self-knowledge needed to drive you toward being your best self. Your values give you a surge of clarity in defining your life's mission, then creating, choo- sing, and implementing actions to drive you towards accomplishing your goals.

How Do Values Tie to Solutions?

By aligning your values to your solutions, you can confidently select the most effective resolution to mitigate each challenge that comes your way.

How Do Values-Driven Solutions Yie to My Energy?

When you are living your life aligned with your genuine values, you gain confidence to make focused choices that bring you energy versus causing you stress.

What Values Do You Resonate with the Most?

Please review the list of values below. Circle 3-5 values that you align with the most. If you have a value(s) that you do not see on the list, feel free to add it.

Abundance	Beauty	Control
Accomplishment	Belonging	Courage
Accountability	Caring	Creativity
Achievement	Clarity	Diversity
Adventure	Commitment	Efficiency
Altruism	Communication	Emotional Health
Authenticity	Community	Empathy
Autonomy	Connecting to	Excellence
Balance	Others	Family

Fitness	Love	Sincerity
Flexibility	Loyalty	Security
Forgiveness	Nature	Self-Realization
Freedom	Openness	Self-Care
Friendship	Optimism	Self-Expression
Fulfillment	Orderliness	Self-Mastery
Fun	Partnership	Sensuality
Giving Back	Patience	Serenity
Gratitude	Peace	Service
Health	Perseverance	Spirituality
Honesty	Personal Growth	Teamwork
Hope	Physical Appearance	Trust
Humor	Power	Truth
Inclusion	Privacy	Uniqueness
Integrity	Productivity	Vision
Intimacy	Professionalism	Vitality
Intuition	Recognition	Vulnerability
Joy	Reliability	Walk the Talk
Justice	Respect	Wisdom
Kindness	Risk-Taking	Worthiness
Leadership	Romance	Other: _____

Value Name: Place the values chosen from the above table into this column.

Definition: In your own words, define what each value means to you.

Action: How much are you honoring your value? Rate how much you are putting each value into action in your life. (1=never, 10=always).

Value Name	Definition	Action
Example: Walk the Talk	If I say I will do some-thing, I will do it.	10

Take a moment and write down a recent challenge you have faced. Detail the challenge, the tools you used to create a solution, and the solution you implemented to address this challenge.

_____

_____

_____

In reviewing the above challenge and solution, can you pick out any values you used to create your solution?

_____

_____

_____

In reviewing the above challenge and solution, do you see any values you omitted in creating your solution? If so, which values were not used?

_____

_____

_____

If applicable, why did this challenge become more important than the value? **Ex.** My feeling of obligation towards my work project and meeting my deadline was prioritized over my value of connecting with others. Therefore, I missed a family gathering.

_____

_____

_____

What is a way you could have honored the value that you didn't use? **Ex.** I could have tried for more balance and left the family gathering early to finish my project.

_____

_____

_____

_____

How might honoring your value have changed this past situation? **Ex.** I would not be angry and resentful towards work. I would not feel guilty about letting my family members down.

_____

_____

_____

Now, take a moment and write down a current challenge you are facing:

_____

_____

_____

_____

_____

What values can you use to create a values-aligned solution?

_____

_____

_____

_____

Take a moment and write down a few ideas of proposed values-driven solutions:

_____

_____

_____

What differences did you notice in creating values-driven solutions?

_____

_____

_____

If you have clarity on how you plan to address your current challenge, please detail any action steps and the time line of each step you plan on completing to address this challenge.

_____

_____

_____

Take a moment and write down any additional takeaways or reflections:

_____

_____

_____

_____

_____

Based on what you now know, what will you implement to begin honoring your values moving forward?

_____

_____

_____

_____

_____

_____

Reflections:

Throughout this assessment, you have discovered, defined, and created values-driven solutions. Feel free to use this space to reflect on anything coming up for you.

_____

_____

_____

_____

_____

Thought Provoking Questions:

Are there other areas of your life not in alignment with your values? If so, note how this makes you feel. How does this impact your energy?

Are there any big changes in your life that are coming soon? How can you lean into your values to navigate these changes and make decisions that align with your values? How energized are you feeling about tackling these upcoming changes?

_____

_____

_____

_____

_____

Index